Stockabet 2019:

An A through Z snapshot of 26 influential companies

Stevan Pirkovic

Stockabet 2019:

An A through Z snapshot of 26 influiential companies

For information, contact:

Stevan Pirkovic

(810) 356-5116

Stevan@Pirkovic.com

Cover design by Stevan Pirkovic.
Cover images courtesy of Pixabay.
Book graphics labeled for reuse or are created by the author.

ISBN: 978-0-9961479-4-1 (eBook)
ISBN: 978-0-9961479-5-8 (paperback)

First Edition: January 2020

Contents

Introduction

Stockabet is a spontaneous review of 26 companies whose stock is publicly traded on major exchanges in the United States. There are two criteria for selection of stock in the 2019 Stockabet list. First, the company's name and ticker symbol must begin with the same letter. And secondly, the company's annual reports and financial disclosures must be as clear and understansdable as possible.

As the name implies Stockabet is organized alphabetically. In order to make the review visually and acoustically appealing, the first letter of the company's name must match the first letter of the company's ticker symbol. For example, we selected Abbott Laboratories, ticker symbol ABT, as the first stock on the list. The first letter in Abbott is "A" and the first letter in the ticker symbol ABT is also "A". We excluded companies that have wordy names like, The Walt Disney Company. Commonly referred to as "Disney", The Walt Disney Company's ticker symbol is DIS, which would have been a contender for the fourth stock on the list. However, Domino's Pizza was choosen instead because the first letter of their ticker symbol DPZ is the letter "D", which matches the first letter of their name "Domino's".

Further narrowing down the list of eligible companies to 26 transparent yet interesting businesses to review was not an easy project. Researching various public companies for this list led to the conclusion that not every company reports their financial statements in the same manner. While many companies in the United States adhere to the Generally Accepted Accounting Principles (GAAP), they still report their financial statements in their own unique way. As a result, most companies file "standardized" reports with the Securities and Exchange Commission, while also publishing "adjusted" or "non-GAAP" figures based on their own internal accounting practices. Sometimes this leads to discrepancies that are difficult to reconcile for an average investor.

Some companies' financial reports are so complex that they require the expertise of professional accountants to interpret. This deterrent ultimately led to the exclusion of several companies from the list.

For example, Fiat Chrysler Corporation, ticker symbol FCAU, was investigated by the Securities and Exchange Commission in 2016 regarding the method in which the automaker reported its sales figures between 2011 and 2016. In some instances, Fiat Chrysler underreported their sales and in others they overreported. Much of the reporting issues was the inconsistent relationship between Fiat Chrysler and their dealer network and what the company considered sales and what dealers consider to be sold inventory.

Another example of inconsistent financial reporting is The Kraft Heinz Company, ticker symbol KHC. The company was subpoenaed by the Securities and Exchange Commission in early 2019 regarding the misreporting of their goodwill and other asset impairments. Kraft Heinz ultimately restated their financial statements for the three year period between 2016 and 2018 as a result of underreporting the cost of their goods sold due to a misinterpretation of their supplier contracts as a result of the company's outdated procurement practices.

Evaluating companies with inconsistent or restated financial reports is difficult, especially on a historical basis. Infamous accounting scandals such as Tyco, Enron, WorldCom, and Valeant Pharmaceuticals have shown that investors often accept or ignore these inconsistencies for long periods of time, often to their detriment. This is why the last seven years of the financial statements were reviewed for companies on the Stockabet list. Income statements, balance sheets, and stock price performance charts were compiled and reviewed for the years 2011 through 2018. While every company is not perfect, there are many who have managed to stay out of the headlines in terms of their accounting practices. The companies selected for Stockabet tend to have easy to understand business models and straightforward financial reports.

1

ABT

Abbott Laboratories

ABT was founded in 1888 and is headquartered in Abbott Park, Illinois. According to ABT's 2018 Annual Report, their primary business is the discovery, development, manufacturing, and sale of a broad and diversified line of health care products.

ABT has five main sources of revenue. Listed in order from largest percentage of income to least, ABT's revenue segments are, cardiovascular and neuromodulation products (30.86%), diagnostic products (24.51%), nutritional products (23.64%), established pharmaceutical products (14.46%), and other (6.52%). Over 65% of ABT's revenues are earned outside of the United States.

Abbott

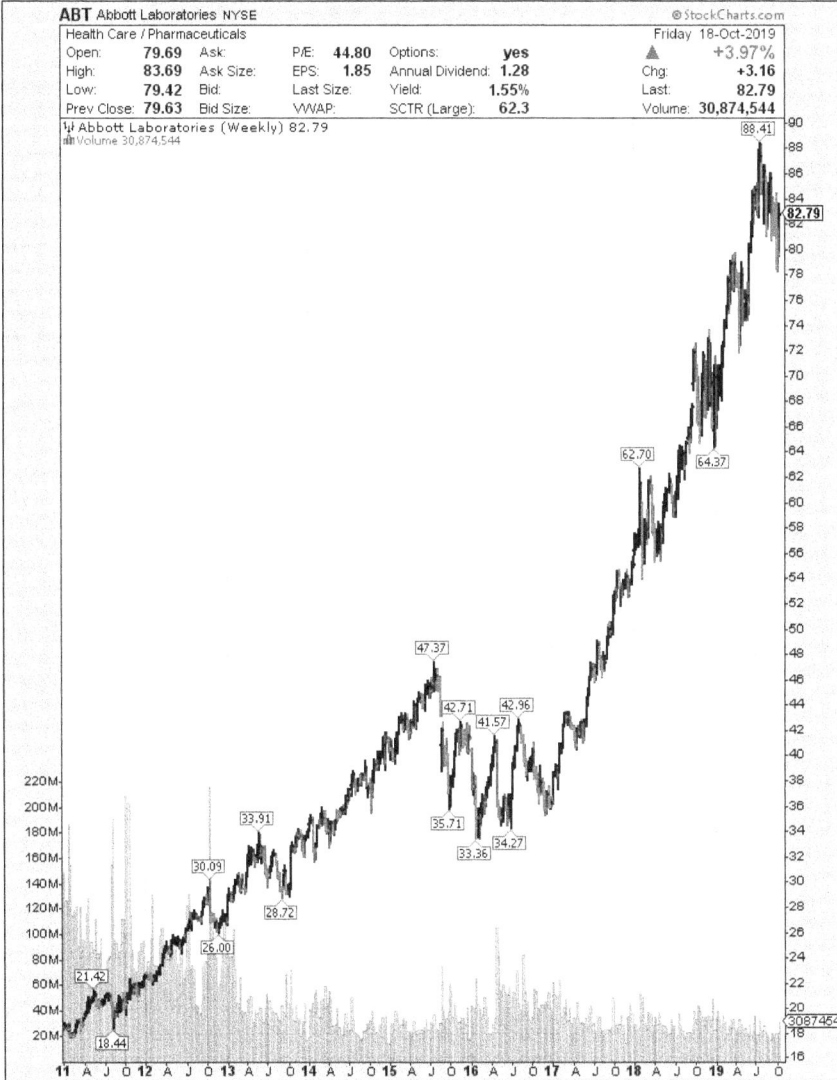

ABT Abbott Laboratories NYSE — © StockCharts.com

Health Care / Pharmaceuticals — Friday 18-Oct-2019

Open:	79.69	Ask:		P/E:	44.80	Options:	**yes**	▲ +3.97%
High:	83.69	Ask Size:		EPS:	1.85	Annual Dividend:	1.28	Chg: +3.16
Low:	79.42	Bid:		Last Size:		Yield:	1.55%	Last: 82.79
Prev Close:	79.63	Bid Size:		VWAP:		SCTR (Large):	62.3	Volume: 30,874,544

ABT stock price chart courtesy of Stockcharts.com

2

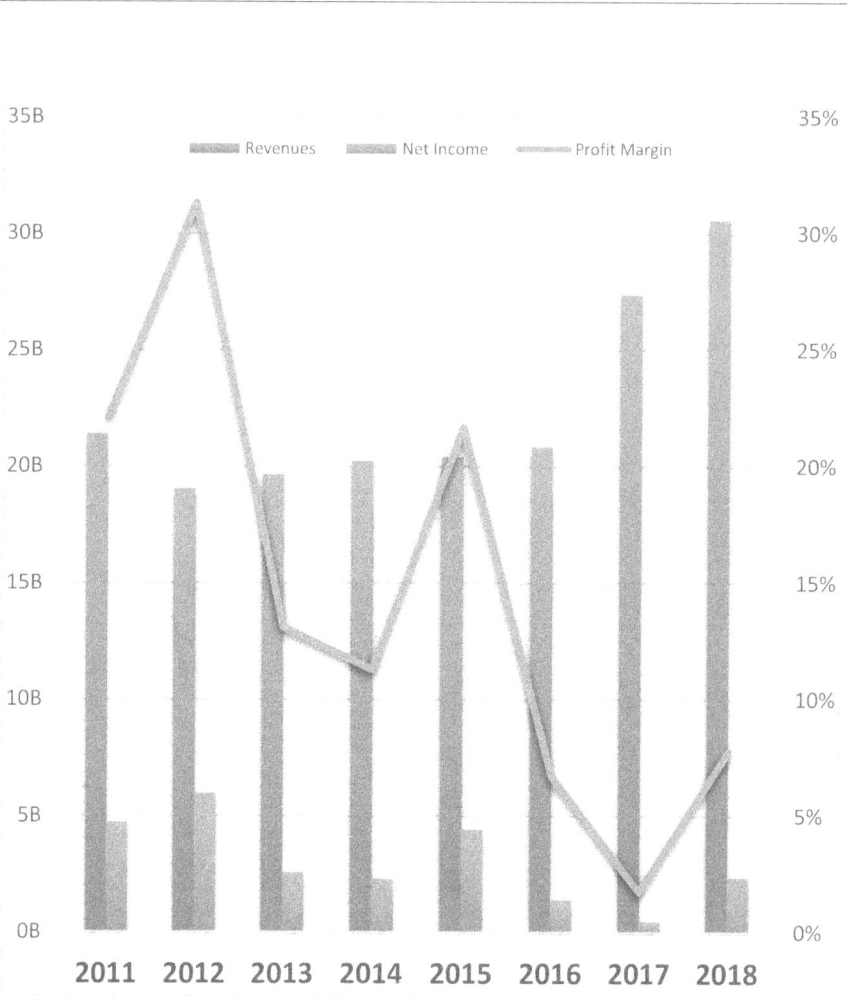

	2011	2012	2013	2014	2015	2016	2017	2018
Revenues	21,407	19,050	19,657	20,247	20,405	20,853	27,390	30,578
Net Income	4,728	5,963	2,576	2,284	4,423	1,400	477	2,368
Profit Margin	22.09%	31.30%	13.10%	11.28%	21.68%	6.71%	1.74%	7.74%

INCOME STATEMENT

ABT

Stockabet 2019:
An A Through Z Snapshot of 26 Influential Companies

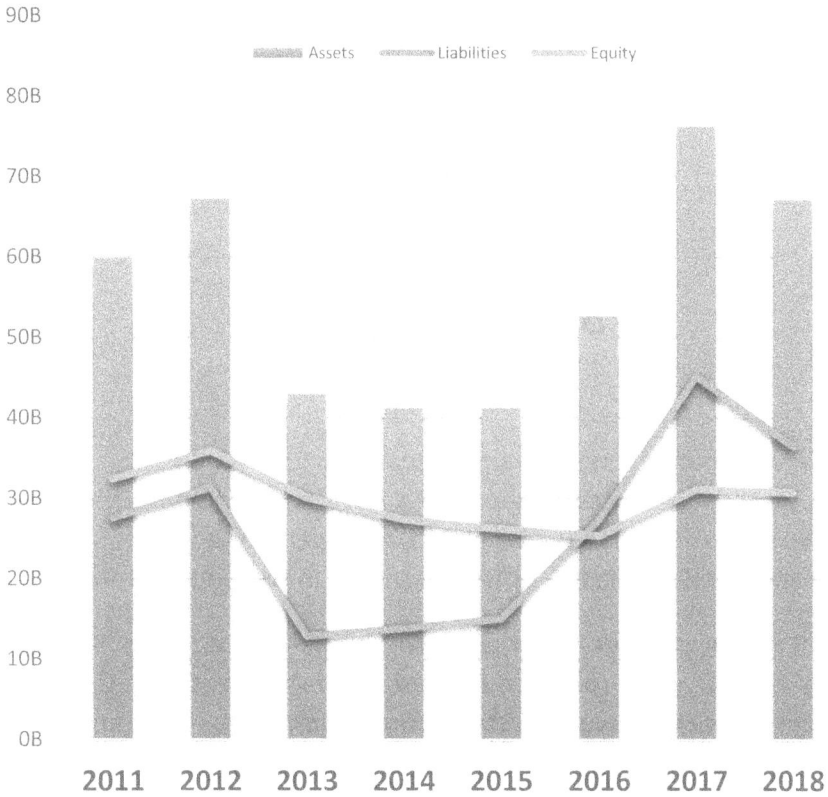

Assets ▬▬ Liabilities ▬▬ Equity

90B								
80B								
70B								
60B								
50B								
40B								
30B								
20B								
10B								
0B	2011	2012	2013	2014	2015	2016	2017	2018

BALANCE SHEET

2011	2012	2013	2014	2015	2016	2017	2018	
59,899	67,235	42,953	41,207	41,247	52,666	76,250	67,173	**Assets**
27,520	31,365	12,895	13,860	15,057	27,341	45,152	36,451	**Liabilities**
32,379	35,870	30,058	27,347	26,190	25,325	31,098	30,722	**Equity**
								Shares
1,567	1,592	1,574	1,527	1,506	1,483	1,749	1,770	(diluted)
								Book Value
20.66	22.53	19.10	17.91	17.39	17.08	17.78	17.36	(per share)

2011 2012 2013 2014 2015 2016 2017 2018 **ABT**

4

2

BXP

Boston Properties

BXP was founded in 1970 and is headquartered in Boston, Massachusetts. According to BXP's 2018 Annual Report, their primary business is the ownership, management and development of Class A office properties in the United States.

BXP operates in five major cities within the United States, Boston, Los Angeles, New York, San Francisco and Washington, D.C. Their main sources of revenue listed in order from largest percentage of income to least are, leases (92.22%), parking and other (3.95%), management services (2.01%), and hotel (1.81%).

bxp Boston Properties

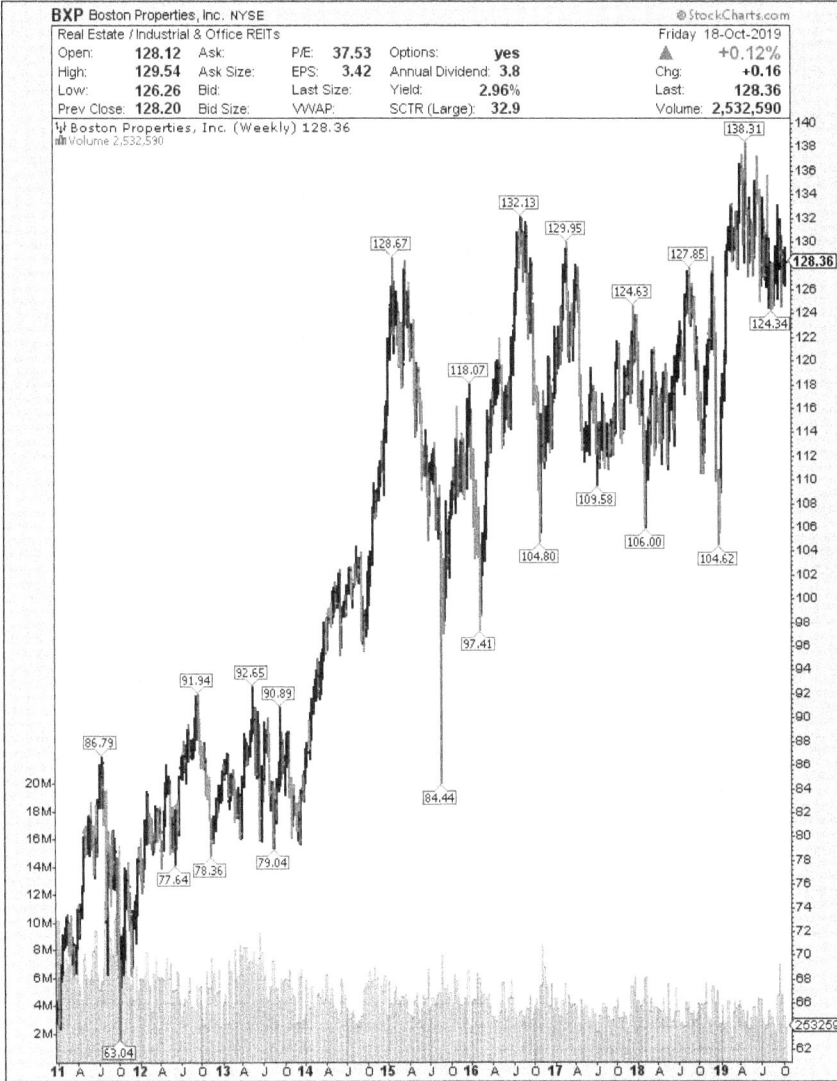

BXP Boston Properties, Inc. NYSE   ® StockCharts.com

Real Estate / Industrial & Office REITs   Friday 18-Oct-2019

Open:	128.12	Ask:		P/E:	37.53	Options:	**yes**
High:	129.54	Ask Size:		EPS:	3.42	Annual Dividend:	3.8
Low:	126.26	Bid:		Last Size:		Yield:	2.96%
Prev Close:	128.20	Bid Size:		VWAP:		SCTR (Large):	32.9

▲	+0.12%
Chg:	+0.16
Last:	128.36
Volume:	2,532,590

Boston Properties, Inc. (Weekly) 128.36
Volume 2,532,590

BXP stock price chart courtesy of Stockcharts.com

6

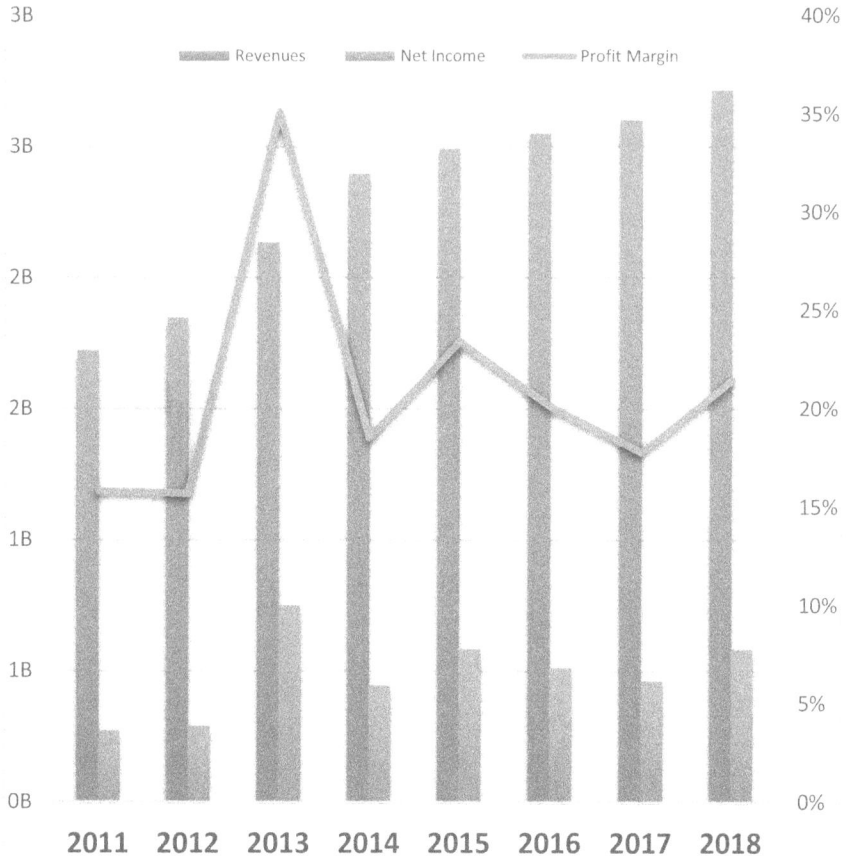

| | Revenues | Net Income | Profit Margin |

INCOME STATEMENT								
1,723	1,847	2,136	2,397	2,491	2,551	2,602	2,717	**Revenues**
273	290	750	444	583	513	462	583	**Net Income**
15.83%	15.68%	35.11%	18.51%	23.41%	20.10%	17.77%	21.45%	**Profit Margin**
2011	2012	2013	2014	2015	2016	2017	2018	**BXP**

Stockabet 2019:
An A Through Z Snapshot of 26 Influential Companies

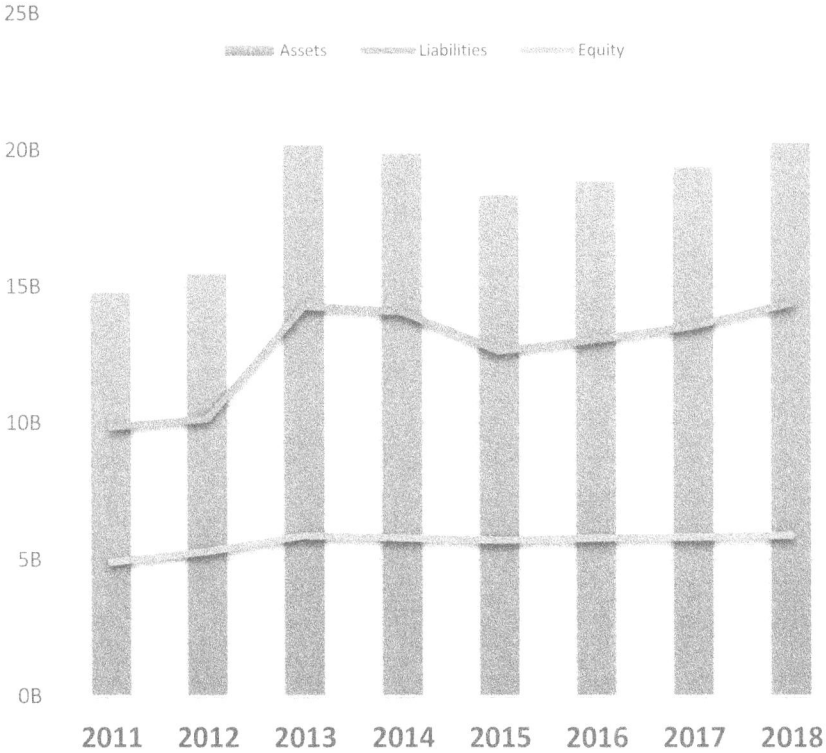

25B

Assets   Liabilities   Equity

20B

15B

10B

5B

0B

| 2011 | 2012 | 2013 | 2014 | 2015 | 2016 | 2017 | 2018 |

			BALANCE SHEET					
14,783	15,462	20,176	19,887	18,352	18,852	19,372	20,257	**Assets**
9,861	10,157	14,284	14,084	12,642	13,065	13,558	14,373	**Liabilities**
4,922	5,306	5,892	5,803	5,709	5,786	5,814	5,883	**Equity**
								Shares
146	151	153	153	154	154	154	155	(diluted)
								Book Value
33.66	35.21	38.64	37.85	37.12	37.57	37.65	38.03	(per share)

BXP

3

CL

Colgate-Palmolive

CL was founded in 1806 and is headquartered in New York, New York. According to CL's 2018 Annual Report, their primary business is the development and manufacturing of personal care products and pet foods. Specifically, CL is the world's leading manufacturer of toothpaste and manual toothbrushes.

CL has four main sources of revenue. Listed in order from largest percentage of income to least, CL's revenue segments are, oral care products (47%), personal care products (20%), home care products (18%), and pet nutrition (15%). Over 70% of CL's revenues are earned outside of the United States.

COLGATE-PALMOLIVE *COMPANY*

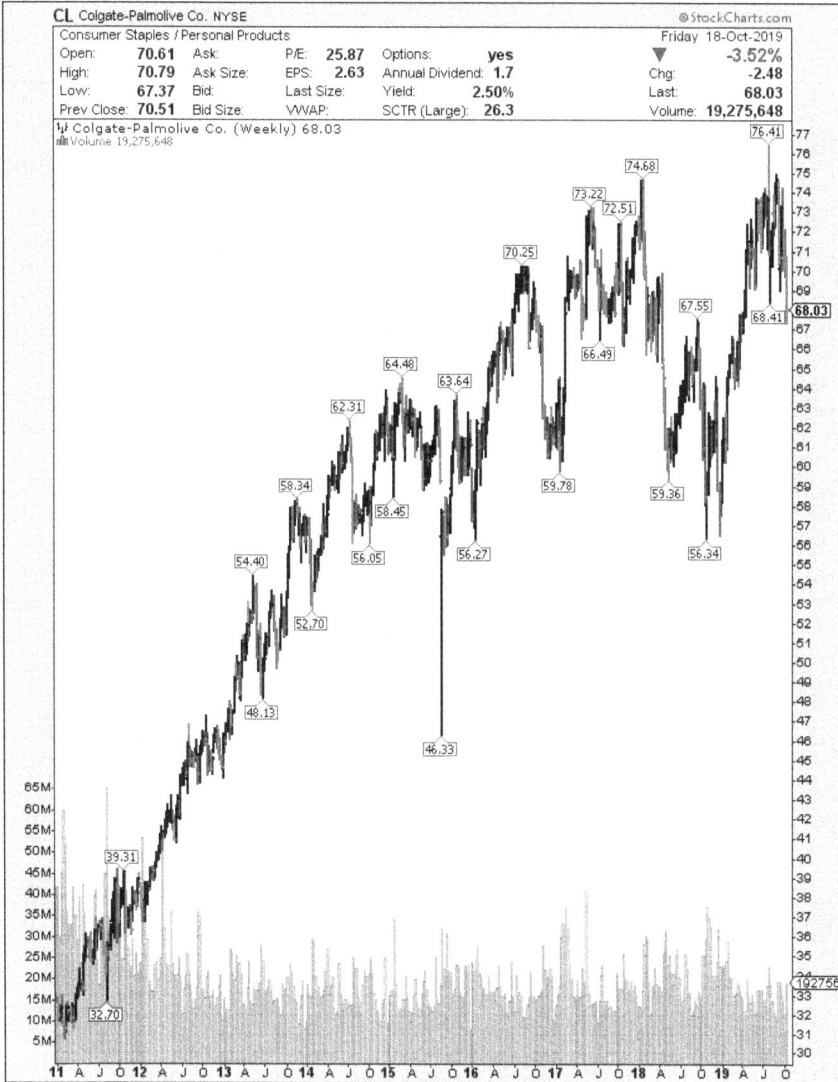

CL stock price chart courtesy of Stockcharts.com

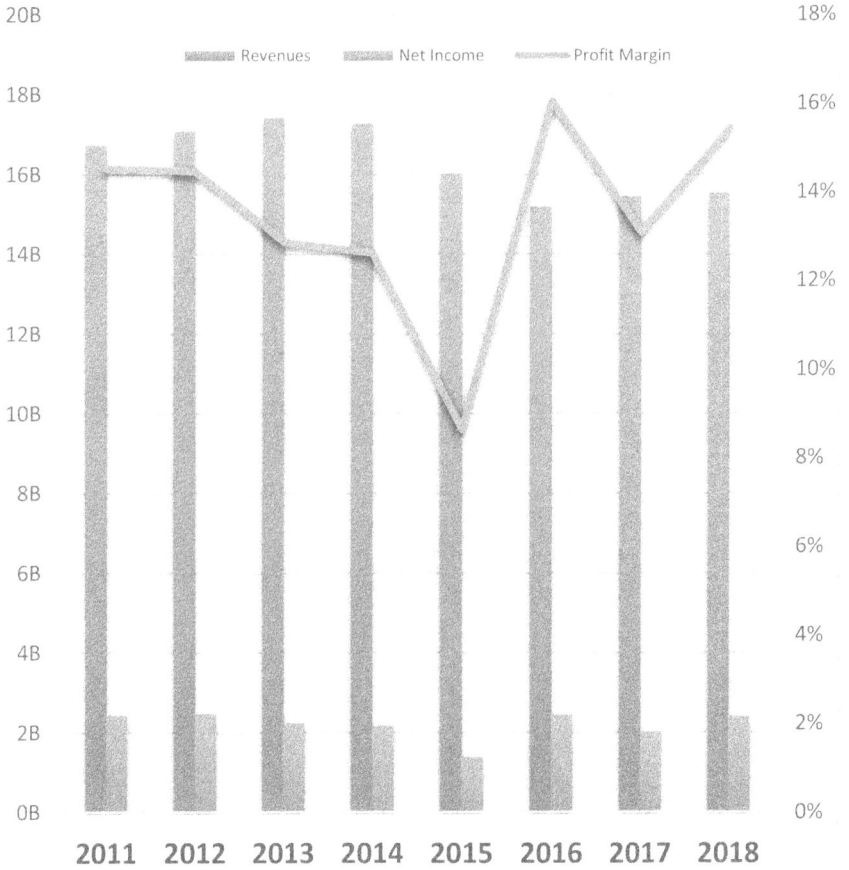

	2011	2012	2013	2014	2015	2016	2017	2018	
	16,734	17,085	17,420	17,277	16,034	15,195	15,454	15,544	**Revenues**
	2,431	2,472	2,241	2,180	1,384	2,441	2,024	2,400	**Net Income**
									Profit
	14.53%	14.47%	12.86%	12.62%	8.63%	16.06%	13.10%	15.44%	**Margin**

Stockabet 2019:
An A Through Z Snapshot of 26 Influential Companies

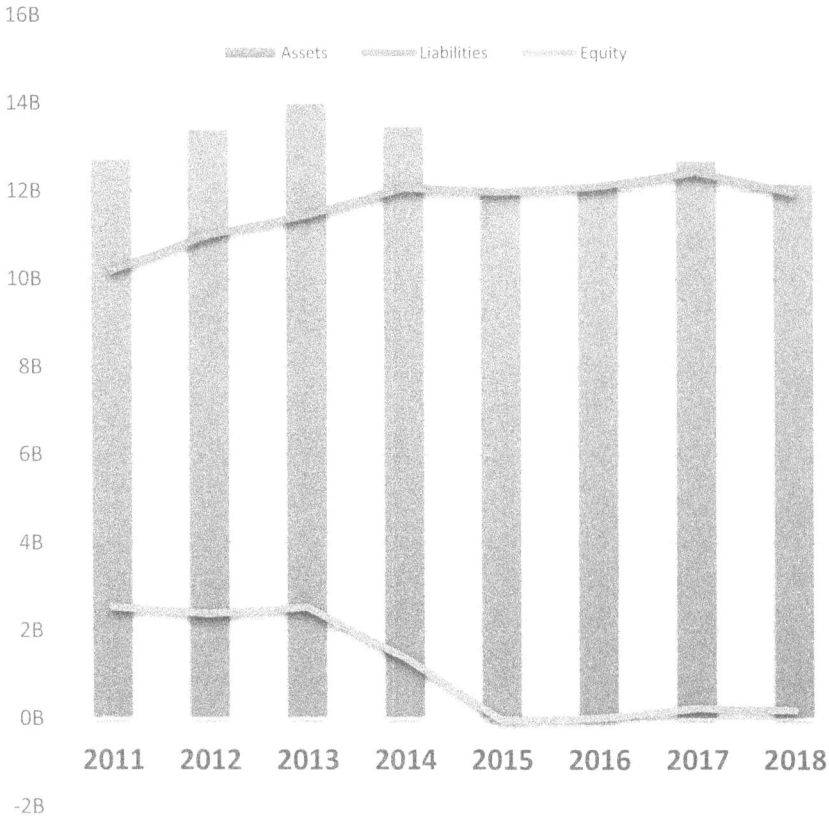

Legend: Assets — Liabilities — Equity

| 16B |
| 14B |
| 12B |
| 10B |
| 8B |
| 6B |
| 4B |
| 2B |
| 0B |
| 2011 2012 2013 2014 2015 2016 2017 2018 |
| -2B |

BALANCE SHEET

2011	2012	2013	2014	2015	2016	2017	2018	
12,724	13,394	13,985	13,459	11,935	12,123	12,676	12,161	**Assets**
10,183	11,004	11,449	12,074	11,979	12,106	12,433	11,964	**Liabilities**
2,541	2,390	2,536	1,385	(44)	17	243	197	**Equity**
								Shares
984	960	940	924	910	898	888	873	**(diluted)**
								Book Value
2.58	2.49	2.70	1.50	(0.05)	0.02	0.27	0.23	**(per share)**

CL

4

DPZ

Domino's Pizza

DPZ was founded in 1960 and is headquartered in Ann Arbor, Michigan. DPZ is the world's largest pizza company based on revenues. According to DPZ's 2018 Annual Report, their primary business is the franchising and the charging of royalties related to the company's pizza products and their associated sales.

DPZ has five main sources of revenue. Listed in order from largest percentage of income to least, DPZ's revenue segments are, supply chain sales (56.61%), U.S. company owned stores (15%), U.S. franchise royalties (11.40%), U.S. franchise advertising (10.44%), and international franchise royalties (6.55%). In 2018 accounting standards adopted in the U.S. resulted in DPZ breaking out royalties it earned which were paid into its national advertising fund. This resulted in DPZ recognizing 10.44% of its revenue as U.S. franchise advertising.

Domino's

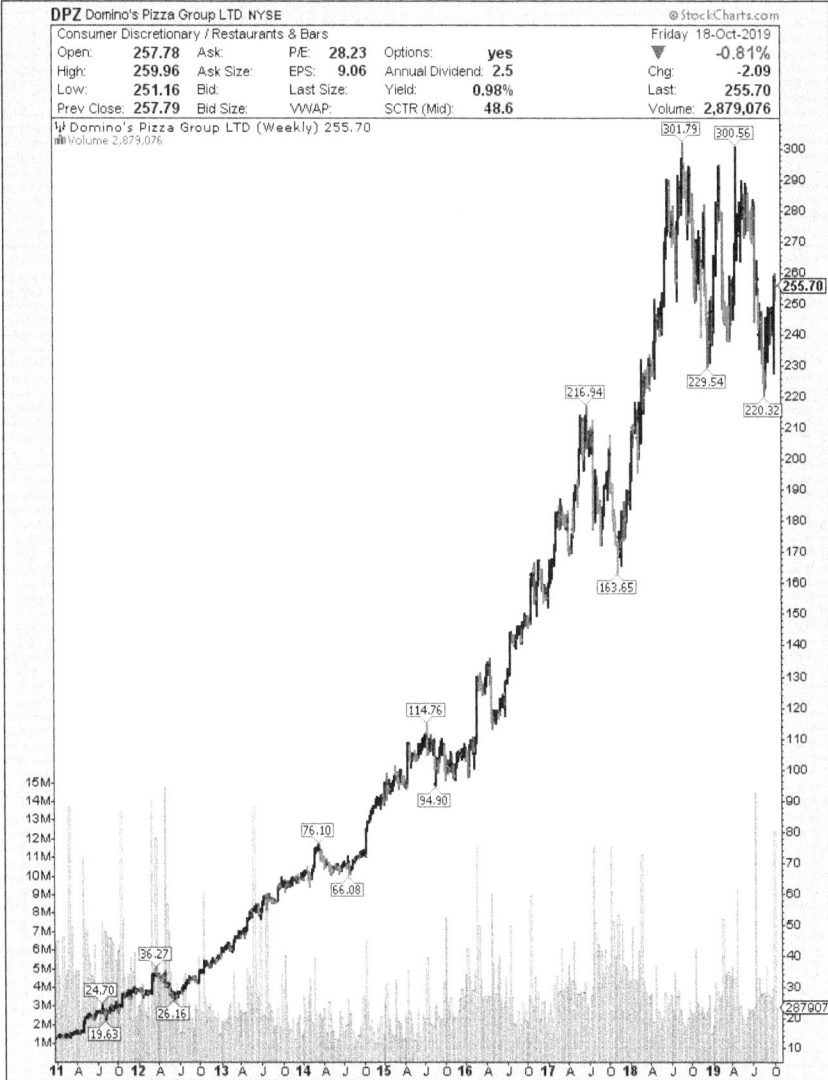

DPZ stock price chart courtesy of Stockcharts.com

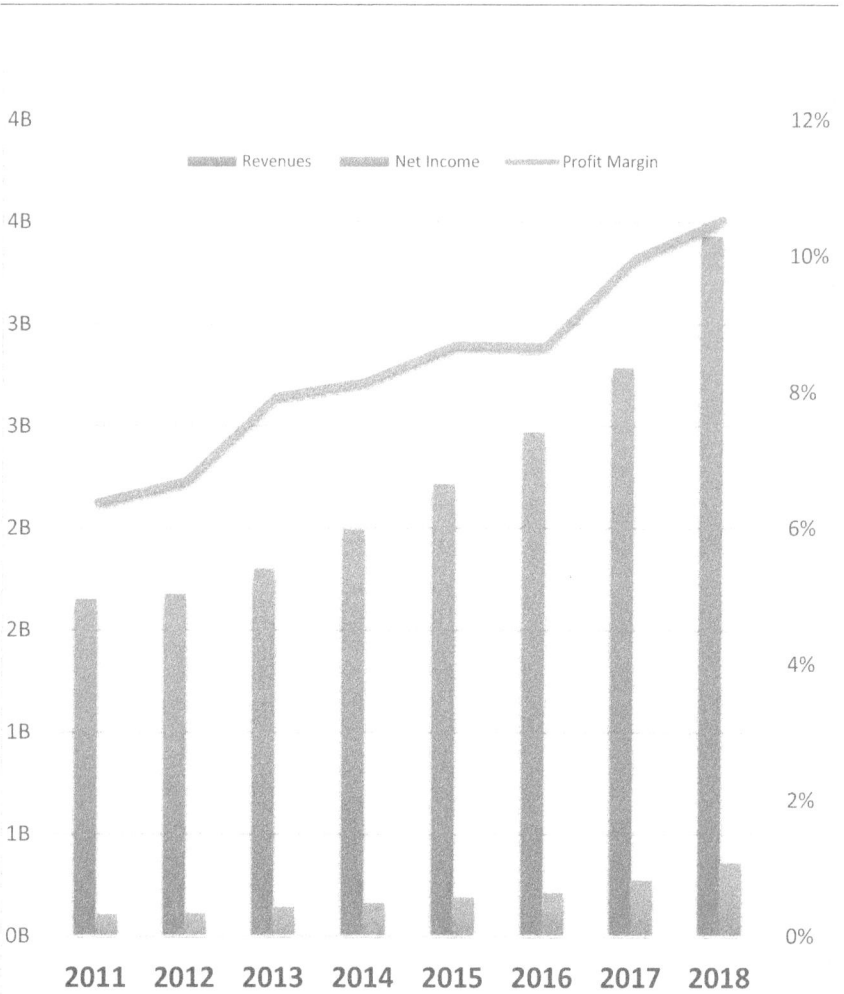

INCOME STATEMENT								
1,652	1,678	1,802	1,994	2,217	2,473	2,788	3,433	**Revenues**
105	112	143	163	193	215	278	362	**Net Income**
6.38%	6.70%	7.93%	8.16%	8.70%	8.68%	9.97%	10.55%	**Profit Margin**

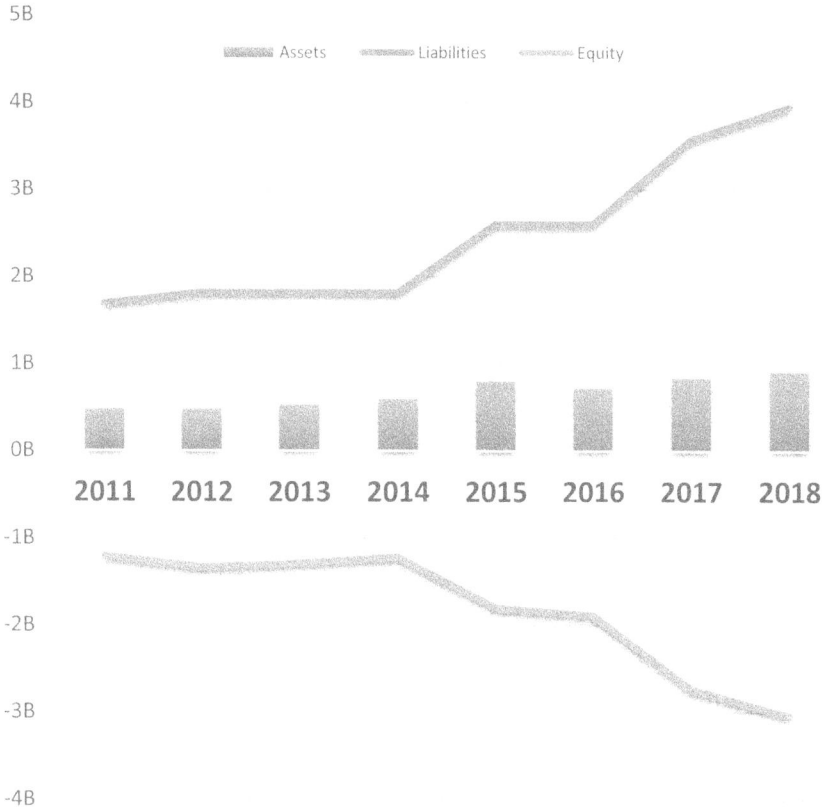

481	478	525	596	800	716	837	907	**Assets**
1,690	1,814	1,815	1,816	2,600	2,599	3,572	3,947	**Liabilities**
(1,210)	(1,336)	(1,290)	(1,220)	(1,800)	(1,883)	(2,735)	(3,040)	**Equity**
								Shares
62	59	58	57	56	50	48	43	**(diluted)**
								Book Value
(19.61)	(22.64)	(22.36)	(21.43)	(32.44)	(37.74)	(57.35)	(70.21)	**(per share)**

DPZ

5

EQR

Equity Residential

EQR was founded in 1993 and is headquartered in Chicago, Illinois. According to EQR's 2018 Annual Report, their primary business is the acquisition, development and management of rental apartment properties located in urban and high-density suburban markets in the United States. EQR wholly owns 287 properties and partially owns 20 properties, with a total of 79,482 apartment units.

Being classified as a Real Estate Investment Trust (REIT), EQR must earn at least 75% of its revenues from real property rents, interest on mortgages, or from the sale of real estate. It must also distribute at least 90% of its taxable income as dividends to its shareholders annually. Additionally, no more than 50% of EQR's shares may be owned by five or fewer individuals or entities, directly or indirectly. As such EQR has only two sources of revenue, rental income (99.97%) and fees (0.03)

Equity Residential

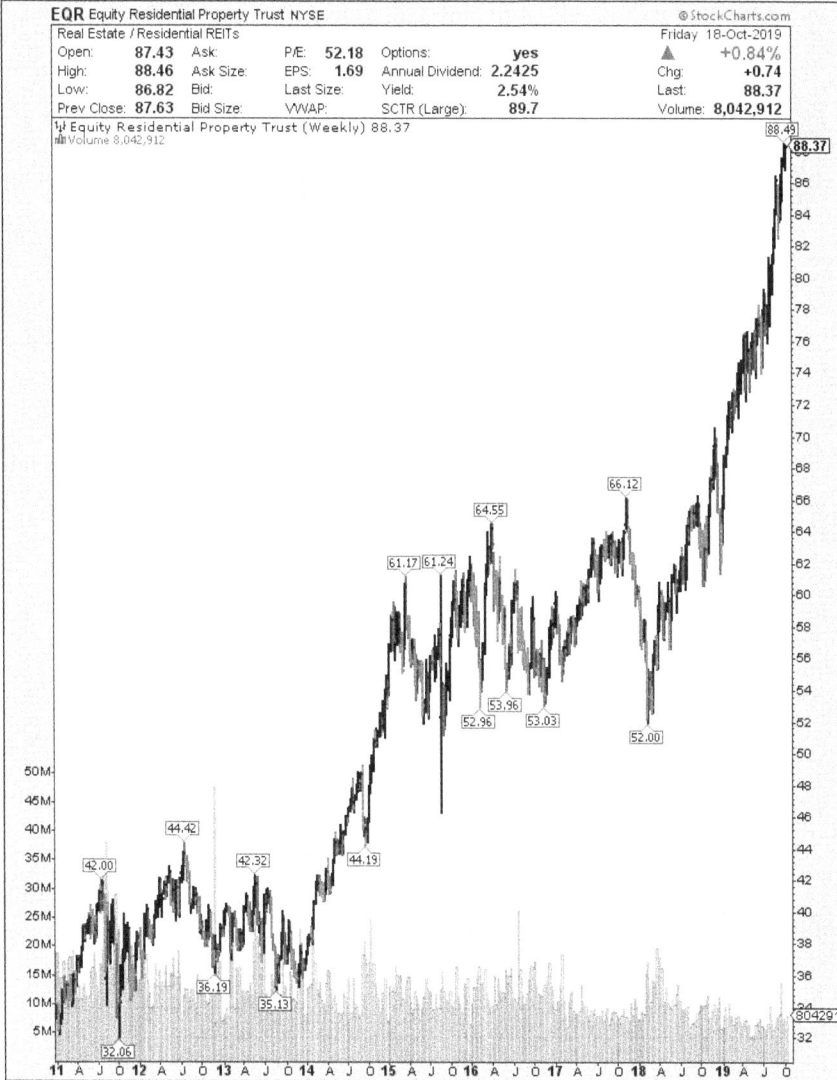

EQR stock price chart courtesy of Stockcharts.com

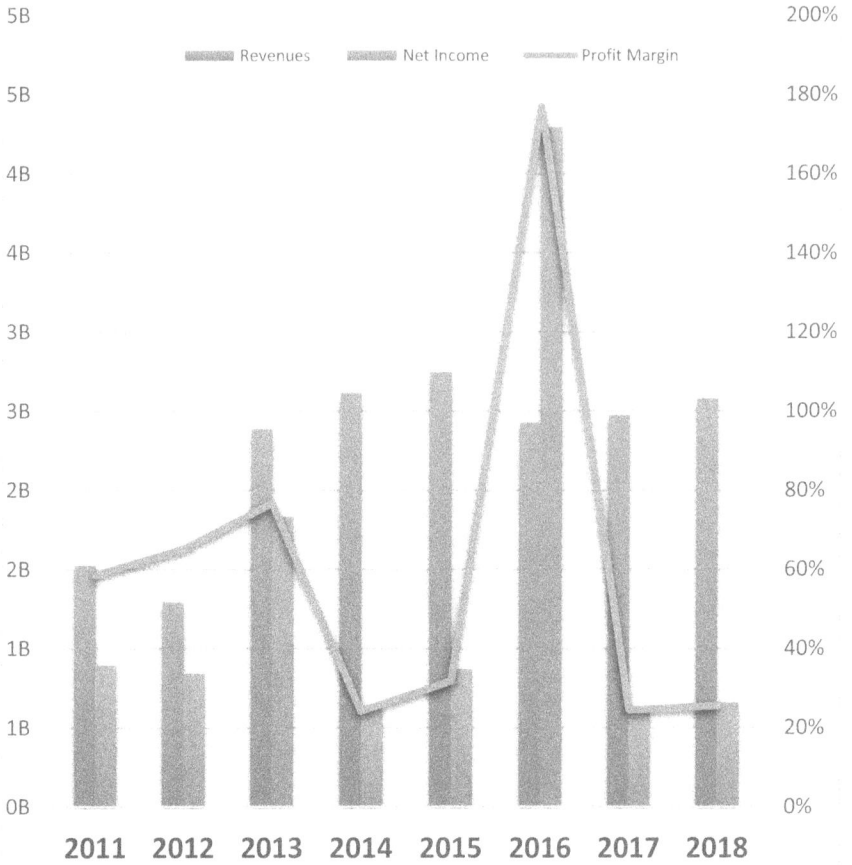

1,525	1,292	2,388	2,615	2,745	2,426	2,471	2,578	**Revenues**
894	842	1,831	631	870	4,292	604	658	**Net Income**
58.59%	65.13%	76.67%	24.14%	31.70%	176.94%	24.42%	25.50%	**Profit Margin**

Stockabet 2019:
An A Through Z Snapshot of 26 Influential Companies

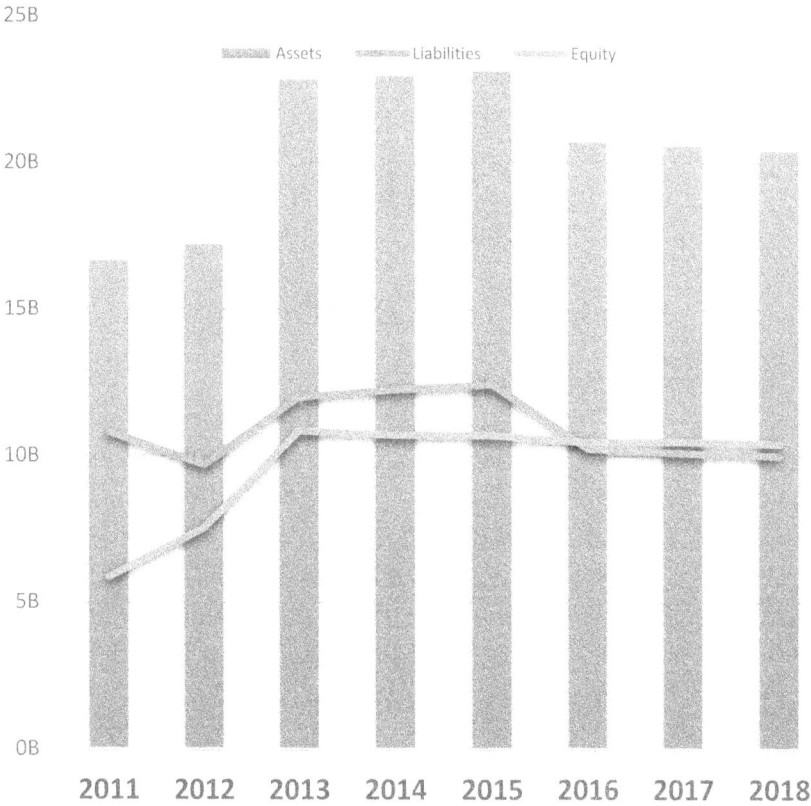

Assets   Liabilities   Equity

| 25B |
| 20B |
| 15B |
| 10B |
| 5B |
| 0B |

2011   2012   2013   2014   2015   2016   2017   2018

								BALANCE SHEET
16,659	17,201	22,835	22,951	23,110	20,704	20,571	20,394	**Assets**
10,796	9,674	11,989	12,243	12,414	10,243	10,097	9,995	**Liabilities**
5,863	7,527	10,845	10,708	10,696	10,461	10,474	10,400	**Equity**
295	320	354	378	381	382	383	384	**Shares** (diluted)
19.88	23.54	30.61	28.35	28.10	27.38	27.37	27.10	**Book Value** (per share)

EQR

6

FNF

Fidelity National Financial

FNF was founded in 1847 and is headquartered in Jacksonville, Florida. According to FNF's 2018 Annual Report, their primary business is the leading provider of title insurance and escrow services in the United States. Most lenders in the U.S. require the use of title insurance in order to complete the funding of real estate transactions. This is to ensure lenders have the priority of lien and that the real estate being mortgaged has a good marketable title.

FNF has five main sources of revenue. Listed in order from largest percentage of income to least, FNF's revenue segments are, direct title insurance premiums (29.25%), agency title insurance premiums (35.42%), escrow fees (28.83%), investment income (0.79%), and corporate income (5.72%). In addition to title and escrow services, FNF is an investor in a variety of software service providers in the mortgage industry.

FIDELITY
NATIONAL FINANCIAL

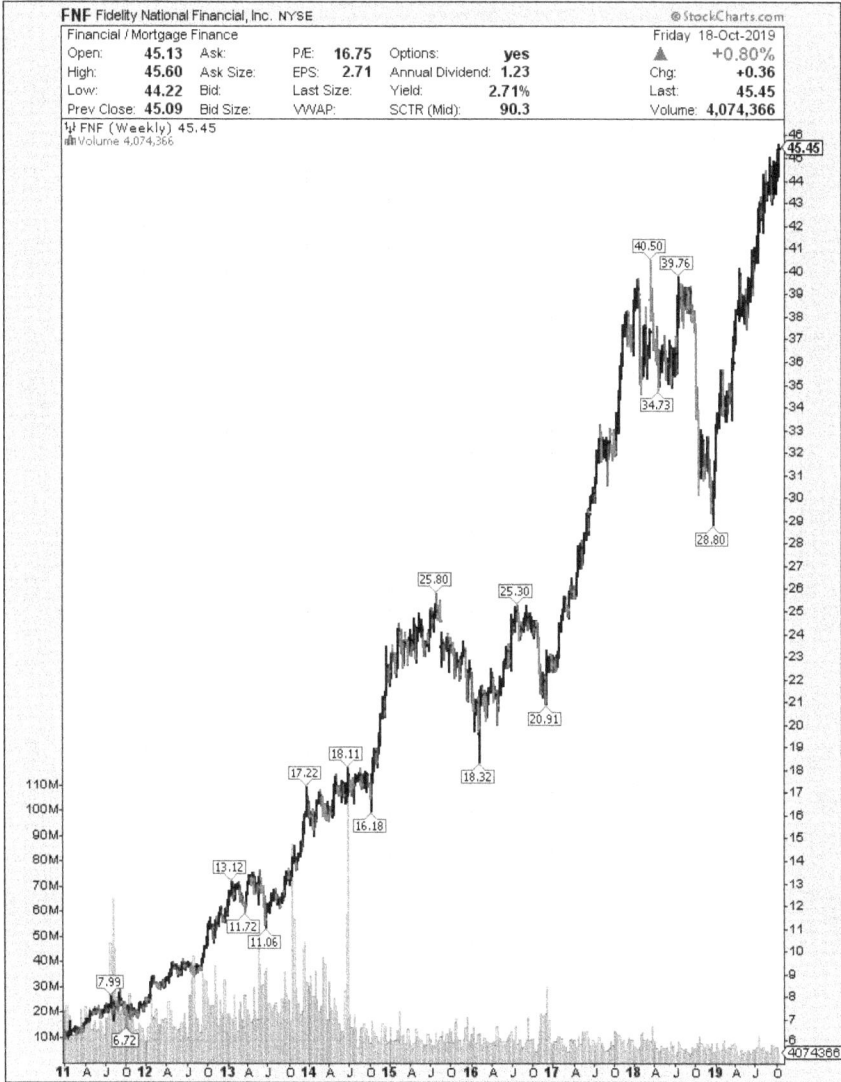

FNF stock price chart courtesy of Stockcharts.com

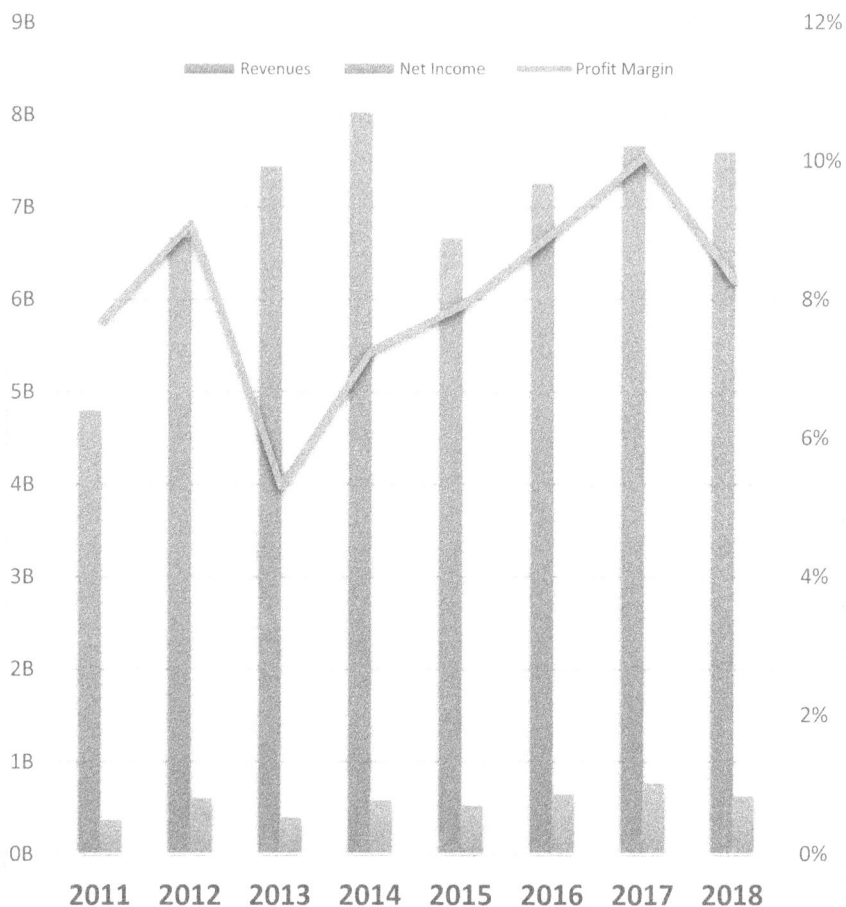

INCOME STATEMENT								
4,800	6,668	7,440	8,024	6,664	7,257	7,663	7,594	**Revenues**
369	607	394	583	527	650	771	628	**Net Income**
7.69%	9.10%	5.30%	7.27%	7.91%	8.96%	10.06%	8.27%	**Profit Margin**

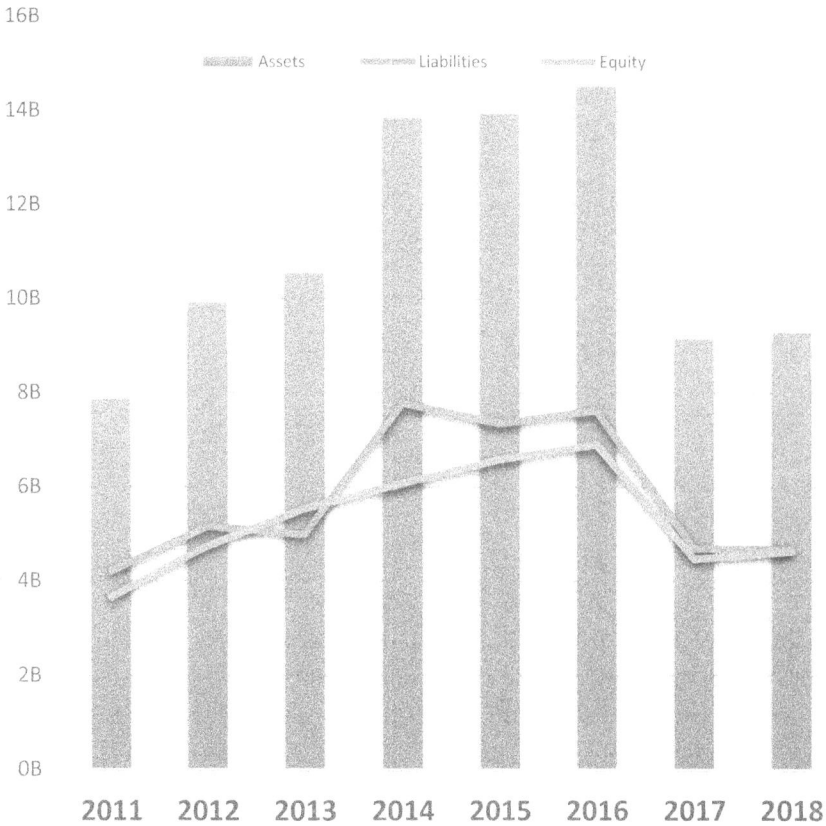

2011	2012	2013	2014	2015	2016	2017	2018	
7,862	9,903	10,528	13,845	13,931	14,521	9,151	9,301	**Assets**
4,206	5,154	4,993	7,772	7,343	7,623	4,684	4,673	**Liabilities**
3,656	4,749	5,535	6,073	6,588	6,898	4,467	4,628	**Equity**
223	226	235	138	368	350	345	278	**Shares** (diluted)
16.39	21.01	23.55	44.01	17.90	19.71	12.95	16.65	**Book Value** (per share)

7

GD

General Dynamics

GD was founded in 1899 and is headquartered in Reston, Virginia. According to GD's 2018 Annual Report, their primary business is the development, manufacturing and sale of a broad range of aerospace and defense products. Specifically, GD produces business aviation products, combat vehicles, weapons systems, munitions, marine systems and provides a wide range of information technology and surveillance services.

GD has five main sources of revenue. Listed in order from largest percentage of income to least, GD's revenue segments are, marine (23.49%), aerospace (23.36%), information technology (22.85%), combat systems (17.24%), and mission systems (13.06%). A majority of GD's revenues are earned from the U.S. government (65%), followed by U.S. commercial customers (14%), non-U.S. government customers (11%) and non-U.S. commercial customers (10).

GENERAL DYNAMICS

GD stock price chart courtesy of Stockcharts.com

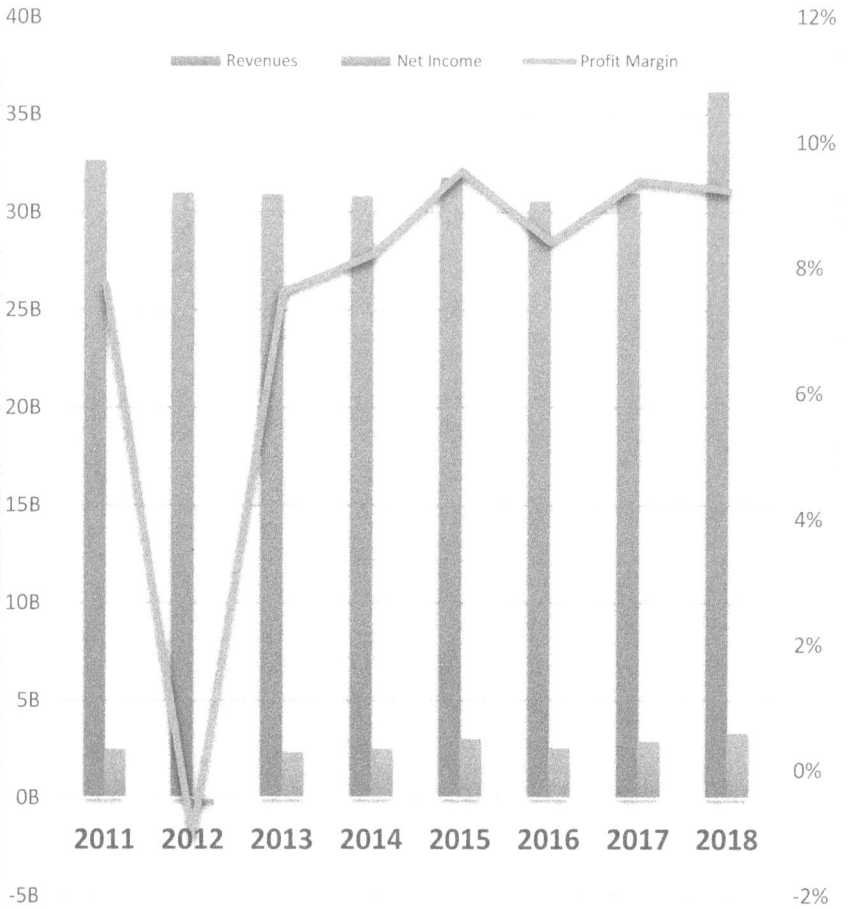

				INCOME	STATEMENT			
32,677	30,992	30,930	30,852	31,781	30,561	30,973	36,193	**Revenues**
2,526	(332)	2,357	2,533	3,036	2,572	2,912	3,345	**Net Income**
7.73%	-1.07%	7.62%	8.21%	9.55%	8.42%	9.40%	9.24%	**Profit Margin**

Stockabet 2019:
An A Through Z Snapshot of 26 Influential Companies

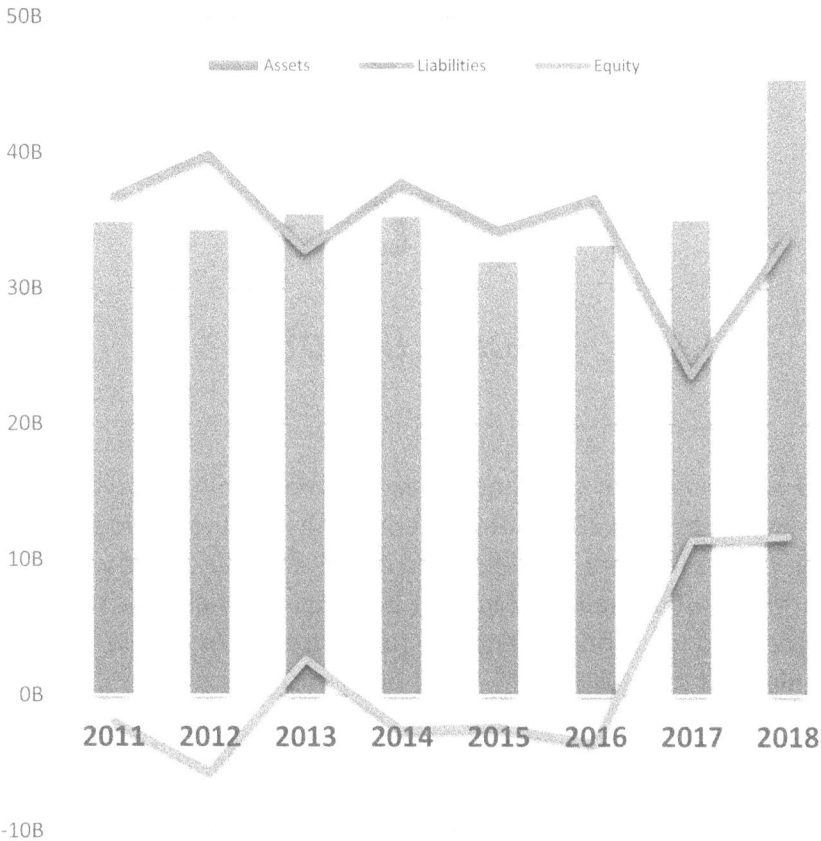

	Assets	Liabilities	Equity

Chart years: 2011, 2012, 2013, 2014, 2015, 2016, 2017, 2018

BALANCE SHEET								
34,883	34,309	35,494	35,337	31,997	33,172	35,046	45,408	Assets
36,784	39,889	32,803	37,861	34,324	36,685	23,611	33,676	Liabilities
(1,901)	(5,580)	2,691	(2,524)	(2,327)	(3,513)	11,435	11,732	Equity
368	353	354	341	327	310	305	299	Shares (diluted)
(5.17)	(15.79)	7.61	(7.40)	(7.12)	(11.32)	37.54	39.21	Book Value (per share)

2011 2012 2013 2014 2015 2016 2017 2018   GD

8

HD

Home Depot

HD was founded in 1978 and is headquartered in Atlanta, Georgia. According to HD's 2018 Annual Report they are the world's largest home improvement retailer based on sales. Their primary business is the retailing of various building materials, lawn and garden products, home décor, installation services, and equipment rental.

HD has three main sources of revenue. Listed in order from largest percentage of income to least, HD's revenue segments are, building materials (36.94%), home décor and appliances (33.49%), and hardware, garden and tools (29.57%). Over 8.15% of HD's revenues are earned outside of the United States.

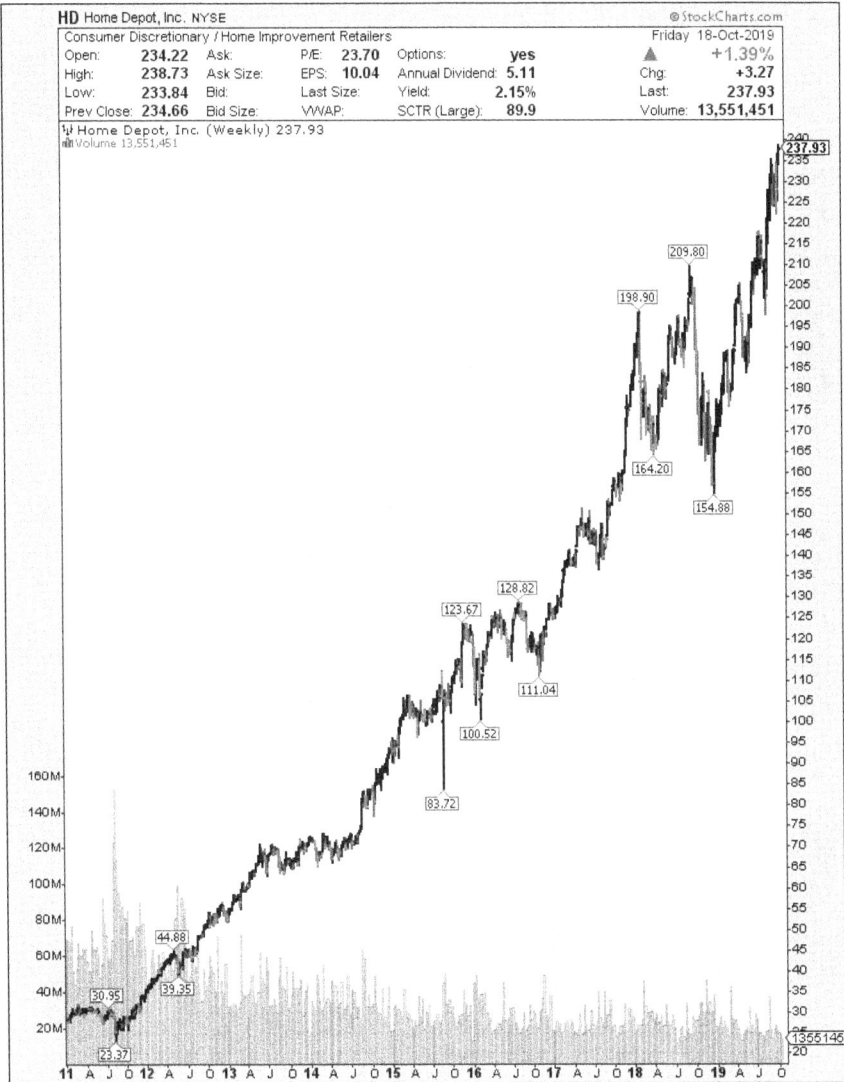

HD stock price chart courtesy of Stockcharts.com

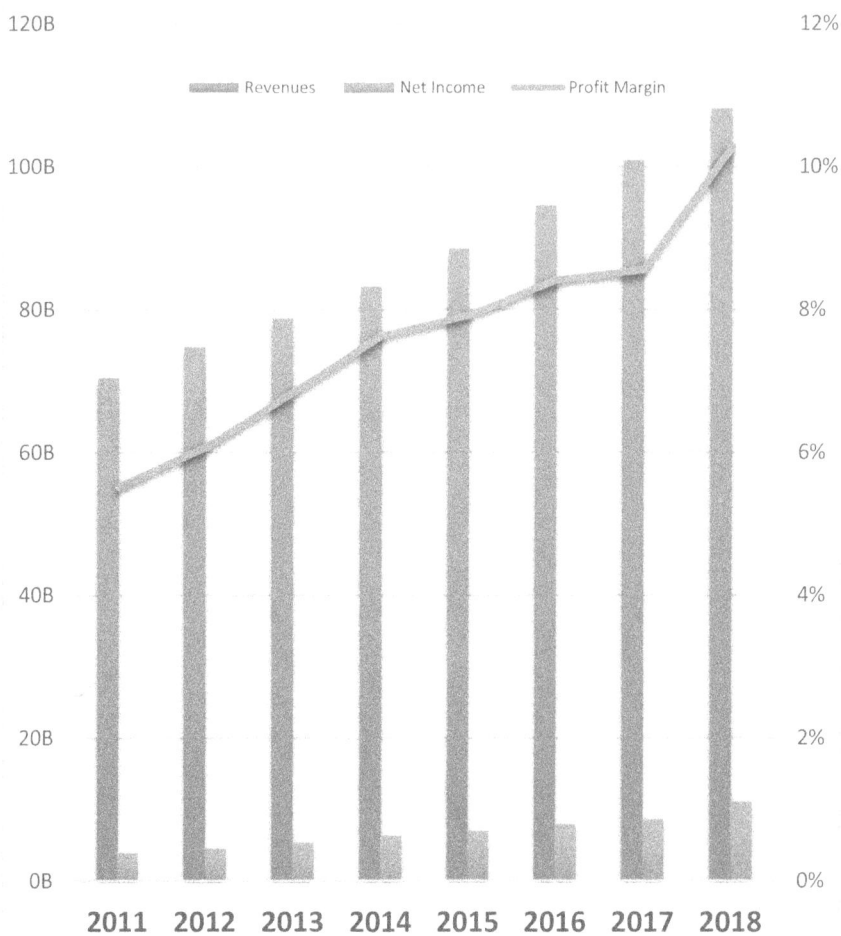

INCOME STATEMENT								
70,395	74,754	78,812	83,176	88,519	94,595	100,904	108,203	**Revenues**
3,883	4,535	5,385	6,345	7,009	7,957	8,630	11,121	**Net Income**
5.52%	6.07%	6.83%	7.63%	7.92%	8.41%	8.55%	10.28%	**Profit Margin**

Stockabet 2019:
An A Through Z Snapshot of 26 Influential Companies

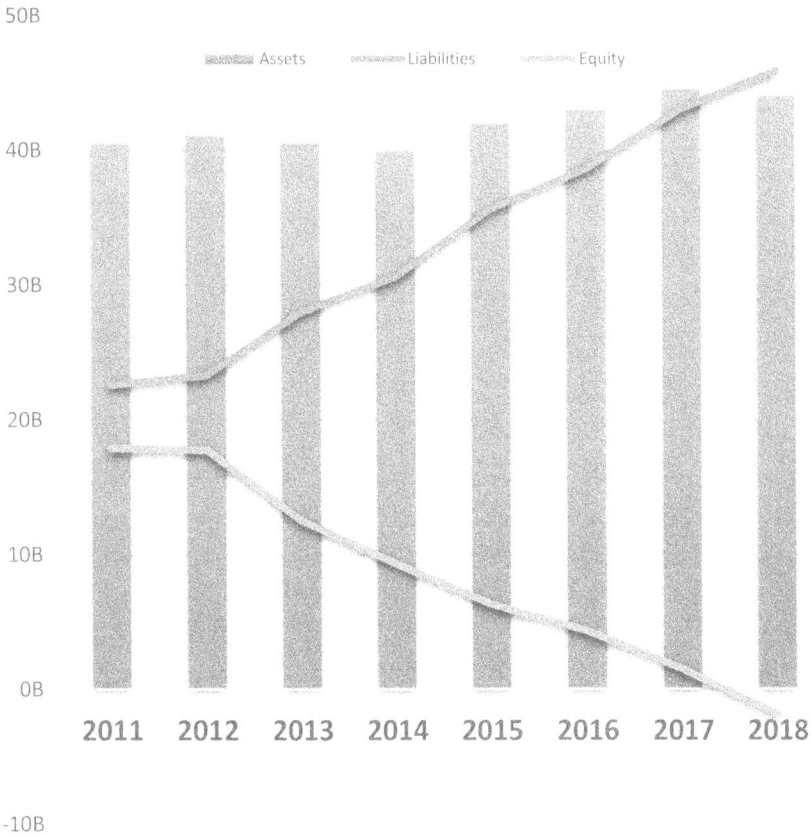

40,518	41,084	40,518	39,946	41,973	42,966	44,529	44,003	**Assets**
22,620	23,307	27,996	30,624	35,657	38,633	43,075	45,881	**Liabilities**
17,898	17,777	12,522	9,322	6,316	4,333	1,454	(1,878)	**Equity**
								Shares
1,570	1,511	1,434	1,346	1,283	1,234	1,184	1,143	**(diluted)**
								Book Value
11.40	11.77	8.73	6.93	4.92	3.51	1.23	(1.64)	**(per share)**

9

IAC

IAC/InterActiveCorp

IAC was founded in 1986 and is headquartered in New York, New York. According to IAC's 2018 Annual Report they are internet media and advertising company. IAC owns mainstream internet websites and mobile applications such as Tinder, Match, Hinge, PlentyOfFish, OkCupid, HomeAdvisor, Angie's List, Handy, Vimeo, Dotdash, Ask.com, Investopedia.com and The Daily Beast. IAC's main businesses are subscription dating products collectively referred to as the Match Group and online market places for home services known as ANGI Homeservices.

IAC has six main sources of revenue. Listed in order from largest percentage of income to least, IAC's revenue segments are, The Match Group (40.58%), ANGI Homeservices (26.56%), Applications (13.66%), Other (12.39%), Vimeo (3.74%), and Dotdash (3.07%). Over 34% of IAC's revenues are earned outside of the United States.

IAC⟋

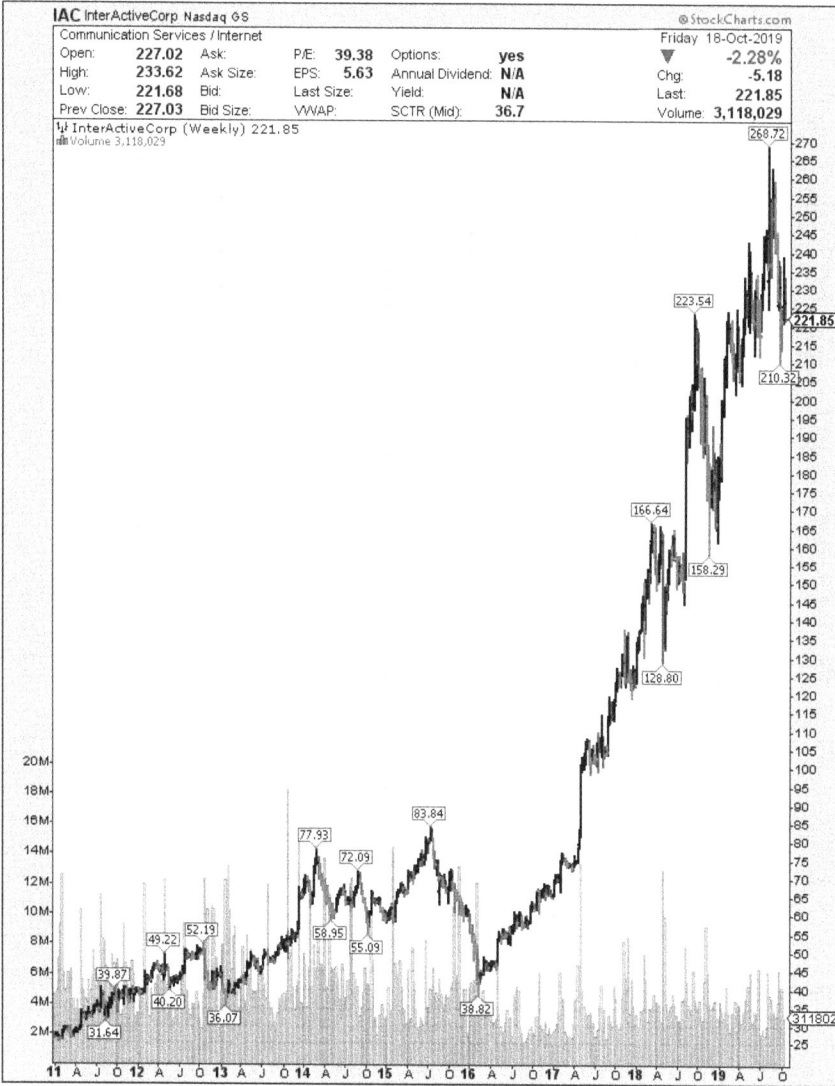

IAC stock price chart courtesy of Stockcharts.com

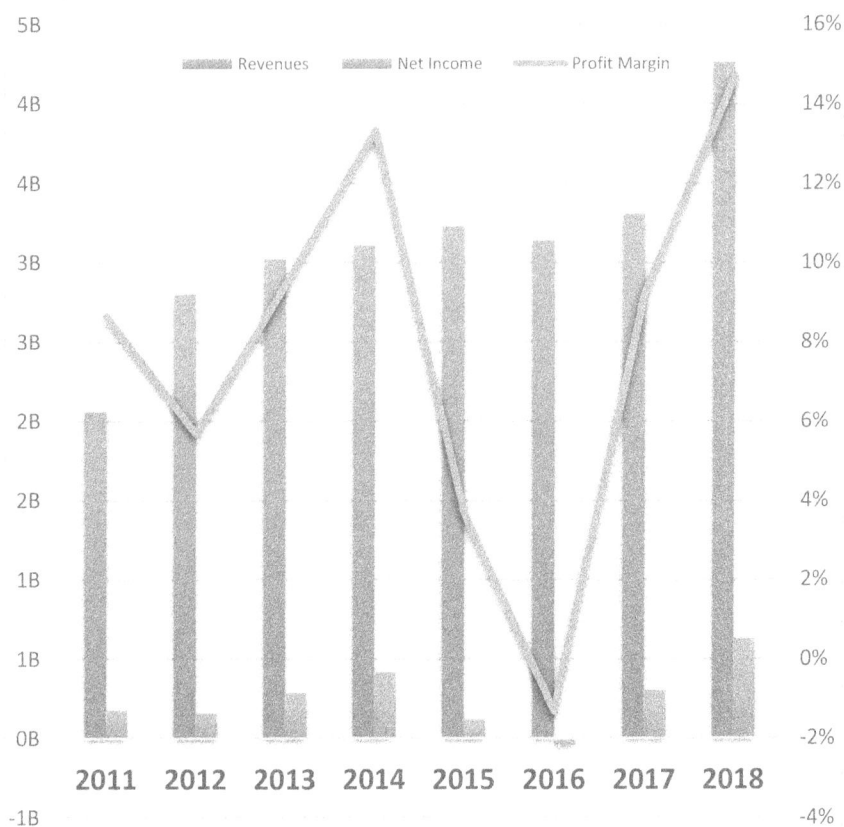

2,059	2,801	3,023	3,110	3,231	3,140	3,307	4,263	**Revenues**
178	159	286	415	120	(41)	305	627	**Net Income**
8.65%	5.69%	9.45%	13.34%	3.70%	-1.32%	9.22%	14.71%	**Profit Margin**

INCOME STATEMENT

Stockabet 2019:

An A Through Z Snapshot of 26 Influential Companies

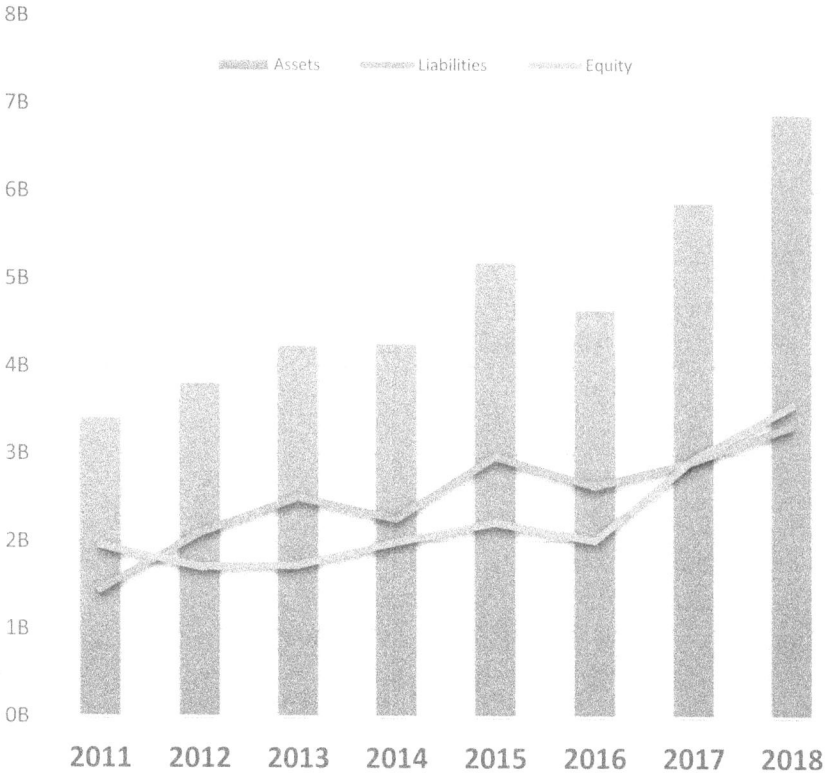

3,410	3,806	4,235	4,257	5,189	4,646	5,868	6,875	**Assets**
1,450	2,098	2,505	2,264	2,973	2,635	2,921	3,323	**Liabilities**
1,960	1,708	1,729	1,993	2,216	2,011	2,947	3,552	**Equity**
								Shares
94	93	87	89	88	80	85	91	(diluted)
								Book Value
20.79	18.34	19.95	22.50	25.09	25.13	34.55	38.90	(per share)

10

JNJ

Johnson & Johnson

JNJ was founded in 1887 and is headquartered in New Brunswick, New Jersey. According to JNJ's 2018 Annual Report, JNJ is a holding company comprised of over 260 subsidiaries engaged in the research, development, manufacturing and sale of health care products across the world. Specifically, JNJ is the world's leading manufacturer of over the counter pharmaceuticals such as Tylenol, Sudafed, Benadryl, Zyrtec, Motrin, and Neosporin.

JNJ has three main sources of revenue. Listed in order from largest percentage of income to least, JNJ's revenue segments are, pharmaceutical products (49.88%), medical devices (33.09%), and consumer products (17.03%). Over 48.66% of JNJ's revenues are earned outside of the United States.

Johnson & Johnson

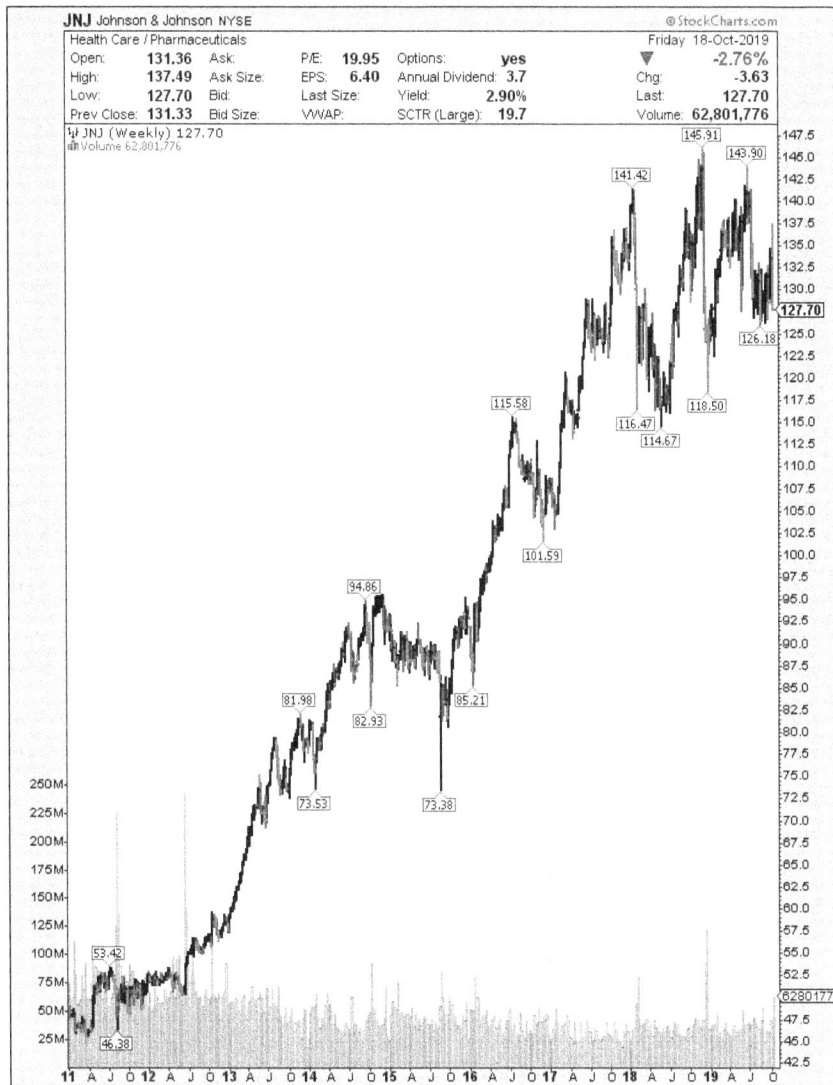

JNJ Johnson & Johnson NYSE						© StockCharts.com
Health Care / Pharmaceuticals						Friday 18-Oct-2019
Open:	131.36	Ask:	P/E:	19.95	Options: **yes**	▼ -2.76%
High:	137.49	Ask Size:	EPS:	6.40	Annual Dividend: 3.7	Chg: -3.63
Low:	127.70	Bid:	Last Size:		Yield: 2.90%	Last: 127.70
Prev Close: 131.33		Bid Size:	VWAP:		SCTR (Large): 19.7	Volume: 62,801,776

JNJ stock price chart courtesy of Stockcharts.com

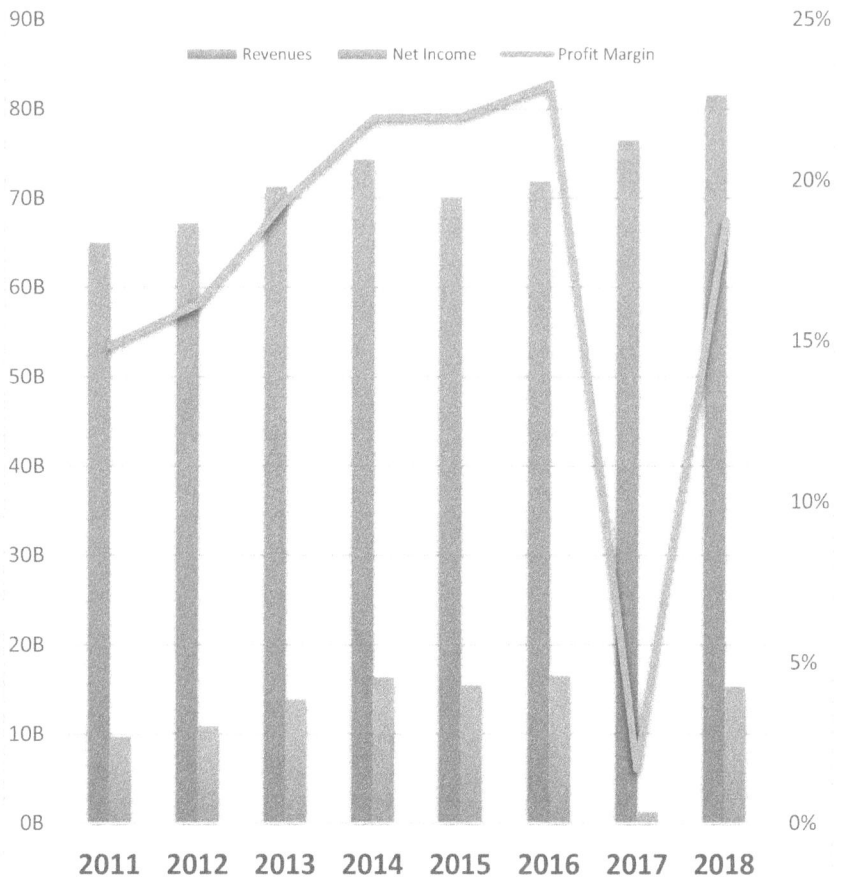

INCOME STATEMENT								
65,030	67,224	71,312	74,331	70,074	71,890	76,450	81,581	**Revenues**
9,672	10,853	13,831	16,323	15,409	16,540	1,300	15,297	**Net Income**
14.87%	16.14%	19.40%	21.96%	21.99%	23.01%	1.70%	18.75%	**Profit Margin**
2011	*2012*	*2013*	*2014*	*2015*	*2016*	*2017*	*2018*	JNJ

Stockabet 2019:
An A Through Z Snapshot of 26 Influential Companies

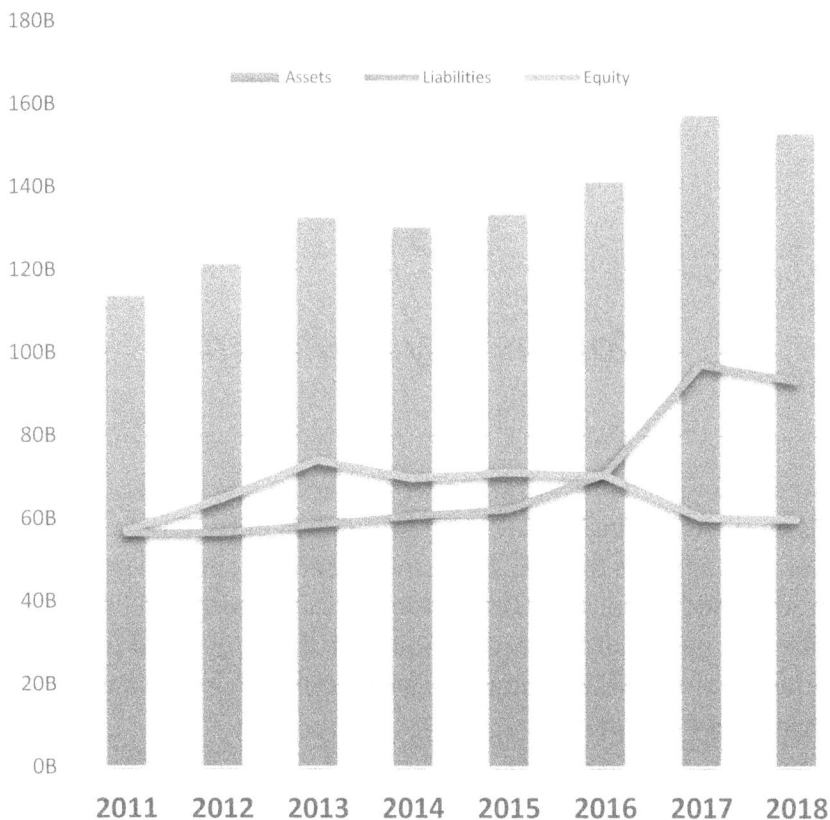

2011	2012	2013	2014	2015	2016	2017	2018	
			BALANCE	SHEET				
113,644	121,347	132,683	130,358	133,411	141,208	157,303	152,954	**Assets**
56,564	56,521	58,630	60,606	62,261	70,790	97,143	93,202	**Liabilities**
57,080	64,826	74,053	69,752	71,150	70,418	60,160	59,752	**Equity**
2,775	2,813	2,877	2,864	2,813	2,789	2,745	2,729	**Shares** (diluted)
20.57	23.05	25.74	24.36	25.29	25.25	21.91	21.90	**Book Value** (per share)

JNJ

11

KSU

Kansas City Southern

KSU was founded in 1887 and is headquartered in Kansas City, Missouri. According to KSU's 2018 Annual Report, KSU primarily operates railroads that serve the midwest and southern regions of the U.S. Additionally, KSU owns railroads in Mexico and Panama under the names of Kansas City Southern de Mexico and the Panama Canal Railway Company, which operate under long-term government concessions.

KSU has seven sources of revenue that correspond to the transportation of various commodities. Listed in order from largest to least percentage of income they are, chemicals (22.92%), consumer products (21.78%), agriculture (17.92%), intermodal (14.10%), energy (9.44%), automotive (9.33%) and other (4.50%). Over 47.50% of KSU's revenues are earned outside of the United States.

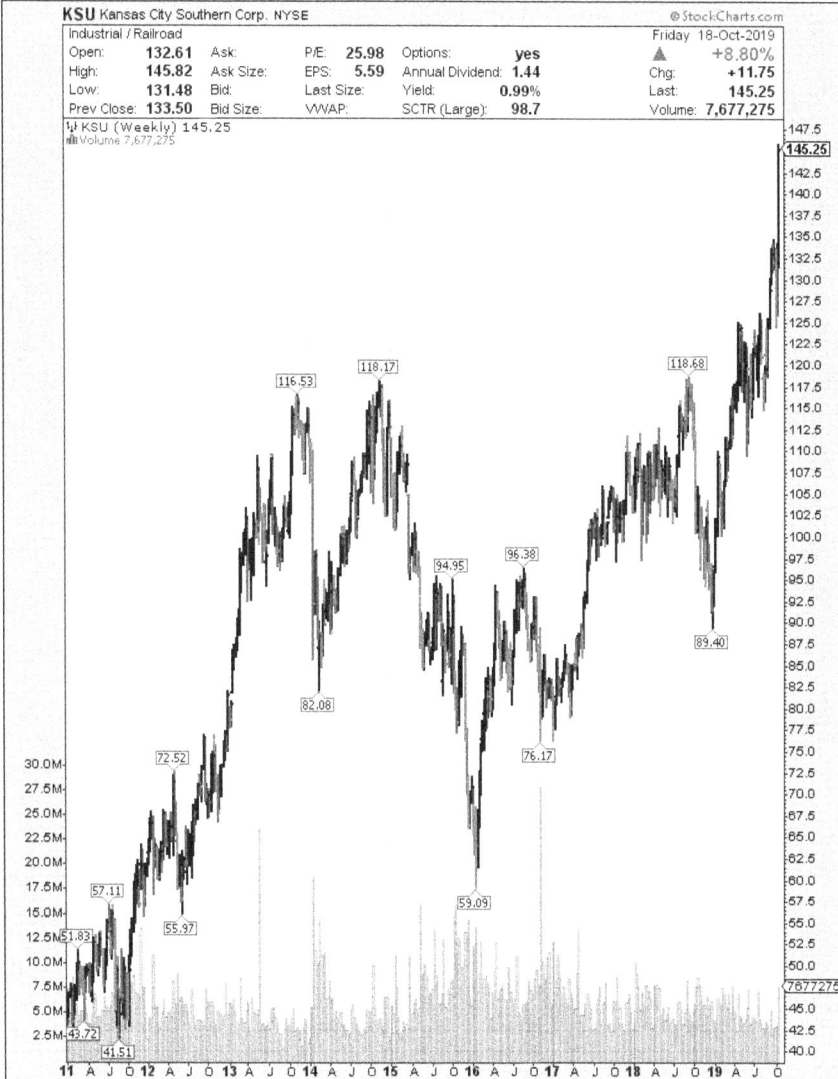

KSU Kansas City Southern Corp. NYSE							© StockCharts.com
Industrial / Railroad							Friday 18-Oct-2019
Open:	132.61	Ask:		P/E:	25.98	Options:	yes	▲	+8.80%
High:	145.82	Ask Size:		EPS:	5.59	Annual Dividend:	1.44	Chg:	+11.75
Low:	131.48	Bid:		Last Size:		Yield:	0.99%	Last:	145.25
Prev Close:	133.50	Bid Size:		VWAP:		SCTR (Large):	98.7	Volume:	7,677,275

KSU stock price chart courtesy of Stockcharts.com

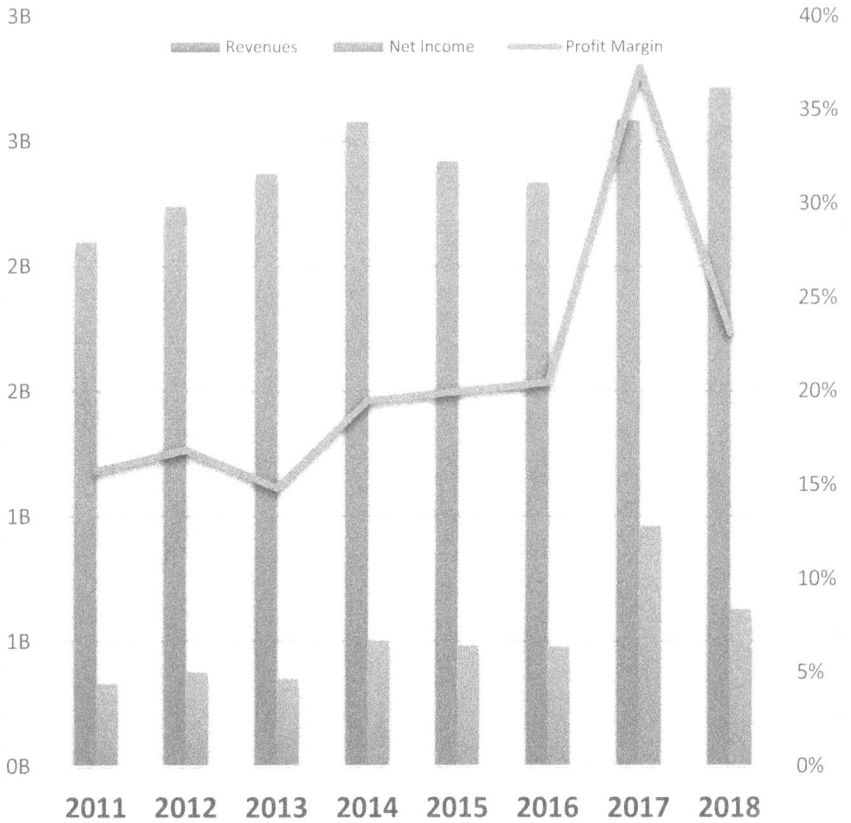

INCOME STATEMENT								
2,098	2,239	2,369	2,577	2,419	2,334	2,583	2,714	**Revenues**
330	377	351	503	484	478	962	627	**Net Income**
15.74%	16.85%	14.83%	19.50%	19.99%	20.48%	37.24%	23.12%	**Profit Margin**

Stockabet 2019:
An A Through Z Snapshot of 26 Influential Companies

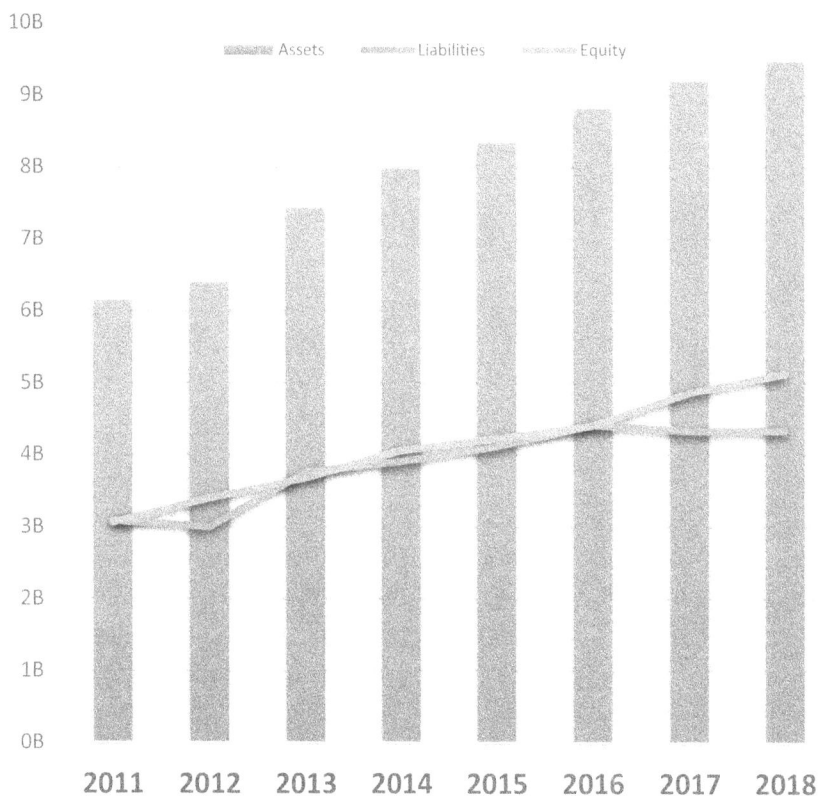

6,145	6,396	7,435	7,976	8,341	8,818	9,199	9,470	**Assets**
3,086	2,995	3,759	3,912	4,116	4,413	4,333	4,337	**Liabilities**
3,059	3,401	3,677	4,064	4,225	4,405	4,865	5,133	**Equity**
								Shares
110	110	110	110	110	108	105	102	(diluted)
								Book Value
27.86	30.89	33.33	36.81	38.44	40.86	46.34	50.17	(per share)

12

LMT

Lockheed Martin Corporation

LMT was founded in 1995 and is headquartered in Bethesda, Maryland. According to GD's 2018 Annual Report, their primary business is the research, design, development, and manufacturing of advance technology systems. Specifically, LMT produces a variety of combat aircraft such as the F-35 Lighting II Joint Strike Fighter, the F-16, the F-22, and the Black Hawk Helicopter, in addition to defense systems, missiles, munitions, and satellites.

LMT has four main sources of revenue. Listed in order from largest percentage of income to least, LMT's revenue segments are, aeronautics (39.23%), mission systems (26.32%), space (18.11%) and missiles (15.63%). Over 28% of LMT's revenues are earned outside of the United States.

LOCKHEED MARTIN

LMT stock price chart courtesy of Stockcharts.com

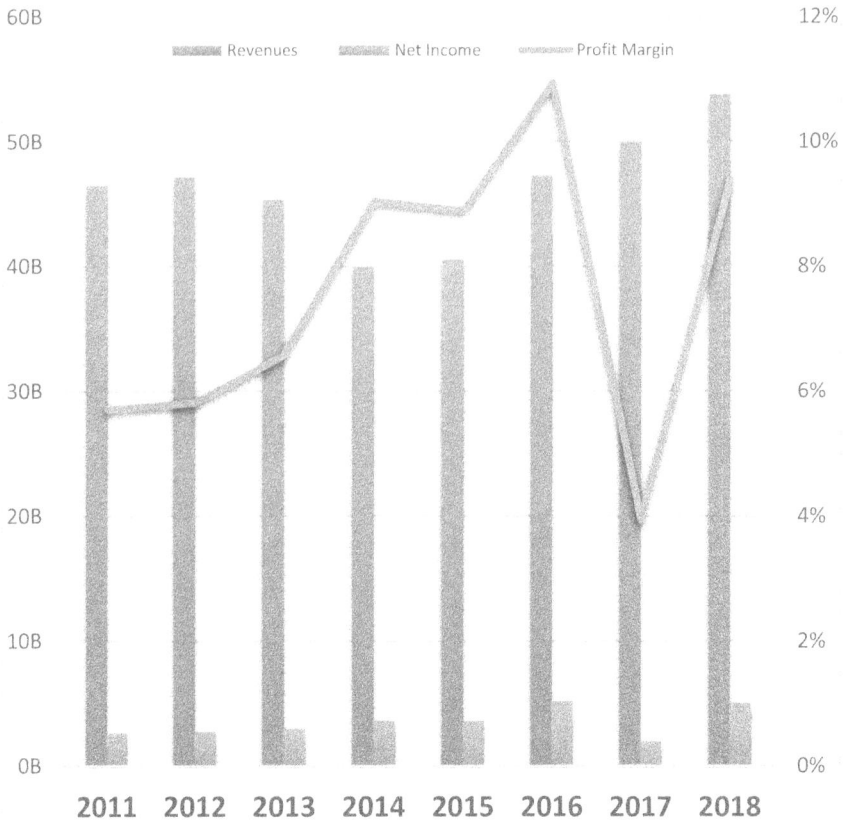

46,499	47,182	45,358	39,946	40,536	47,290	49,960	53,762	**Revenues**
2,655	2,745	2,981	3,614	3,605	5,173	1,963	5,046	**Net Income**
5.71%	5.82%	6.57%	9.05%	8.89%	10.94%	3.93%	9.39%	**Profit Margin**

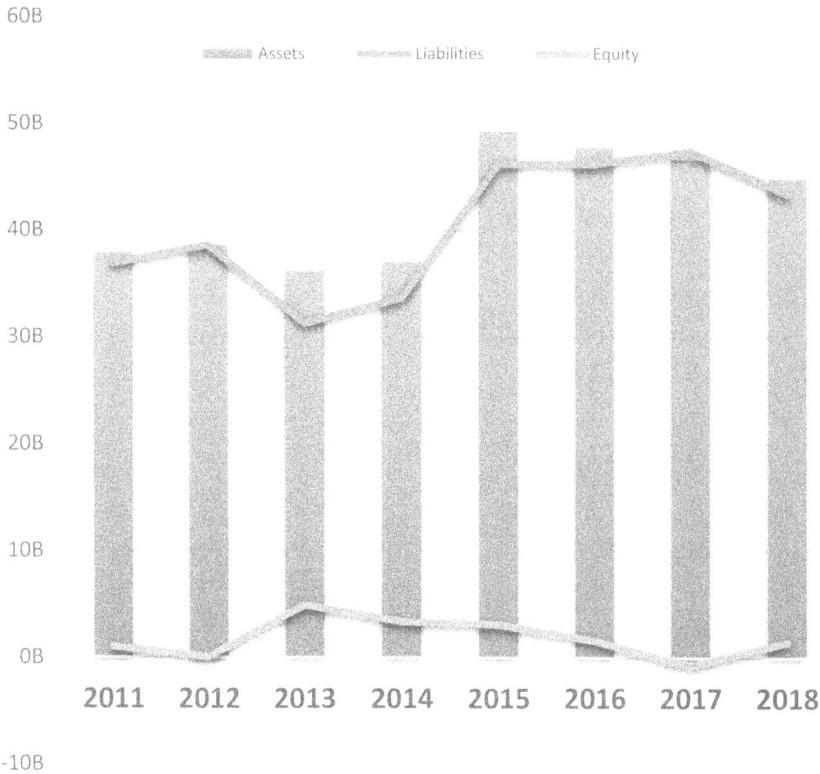

37,908	38,657	36,188	37,046	49,304	47,806	46,620	44,876	**Assets**
36,907	38,618	31,270	33,646	46,207	46,200	47,396	43,427	**Liabilities**
1,001	39	4,918	3,400	3,097	1,606	(776)	1,449	**Equity**
340	328	327	322	315	303	291	287	**Shares (diluted)**
2.94	0.12	15.06	10.55	9.84	5.30	(2.67)	5.05	**Book Value (per share)**

13

MSFT

Microsoft

MSFT was founded in 1975 and is headquartered in Redmond, Washington. According to MSFT's 2018 Annual Report, their primary business is the development and support of software, technology services, operating systems, and business applications. Specifically, MSFT is a global technology company that owns online platforms such as LinkedIn, GitHub and Xbox Live. MSFT also designs, manufactures and sells electronic devices such as personal computers, mobile tablets, gaming consoles, intelligent devices and related accessories.

MSFT has three main sources of revenue. Listed in order from largest percentage of income to least, MSFT's revenue segments are, personal computing (36.31%), productivity and business processes (32.71%), and intelligent cloud (30.98%). Over 48.98% of MSFT's revenues are earned outside of the United States.

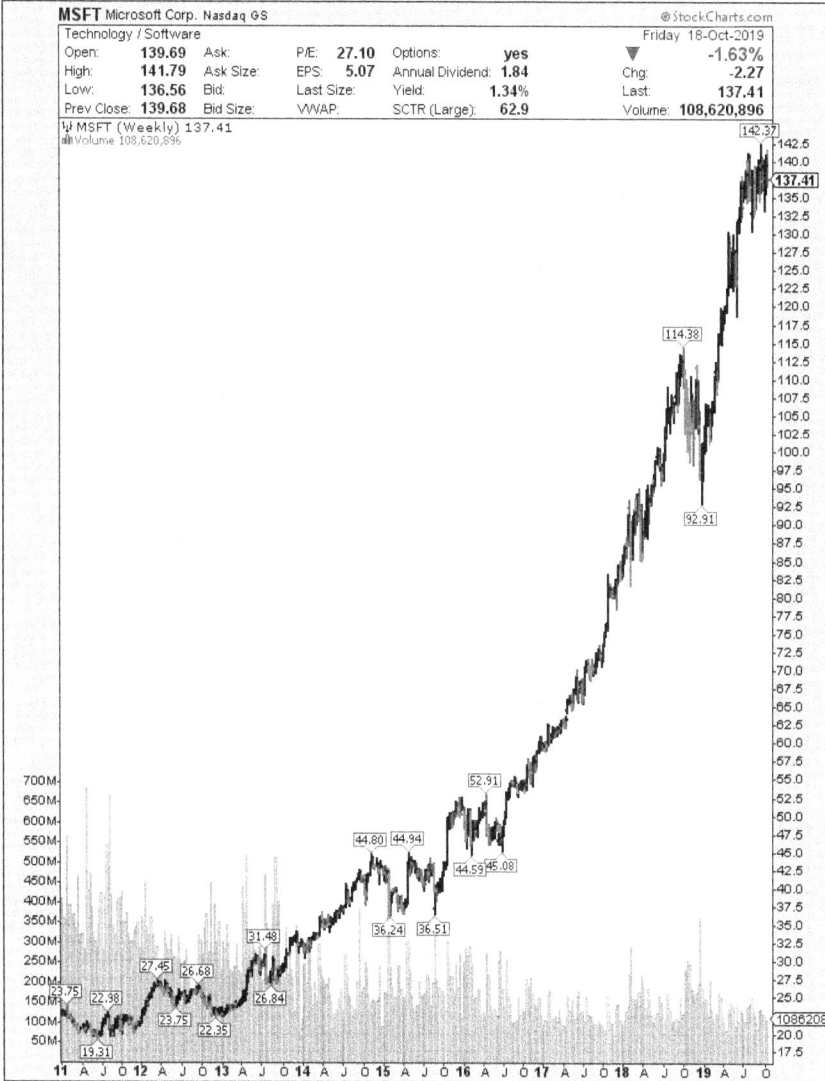

MSFT stock price chart courtesy of Stockcharts.com

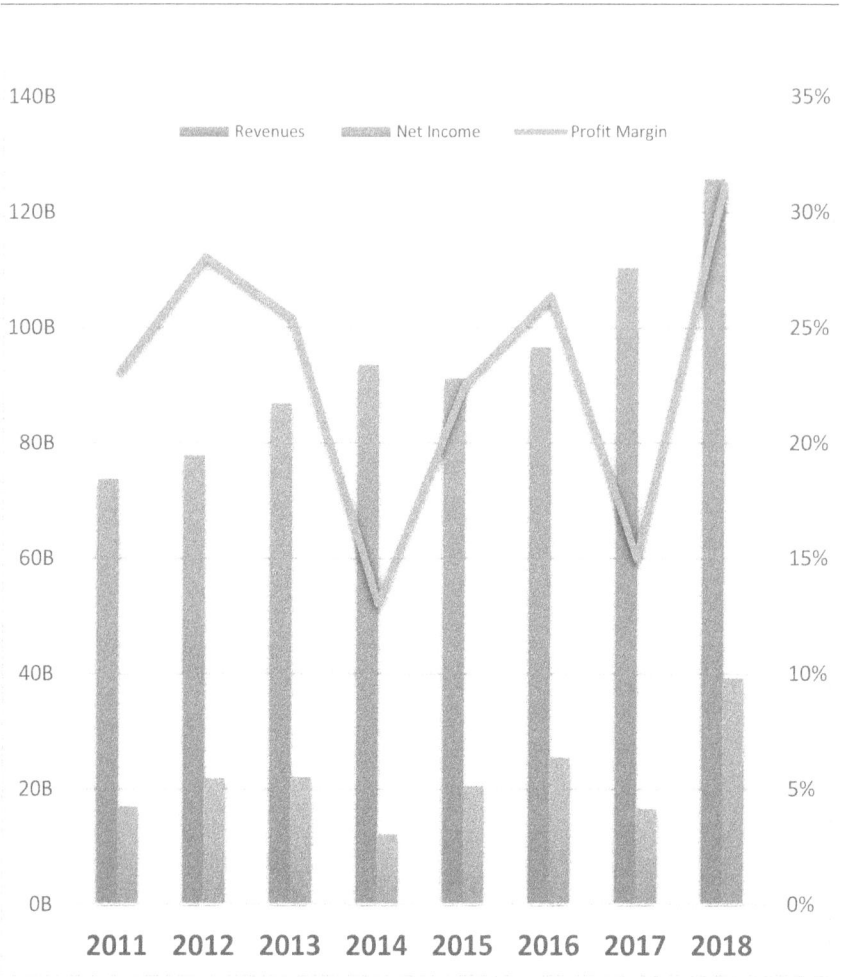

INCOME STATEMENT								
73,723	77,849	86,833	93,580	91,154	96,571	110,360	125,843	**Revenues**
16,978	21,863	22,074	12,193	20,539	25,489	16,571	39,240	**Net Income**
23.03%	28.08%	25.42%	13.03%	22.53%	26.39%	15.02%	31.18%	**Profit Margin**

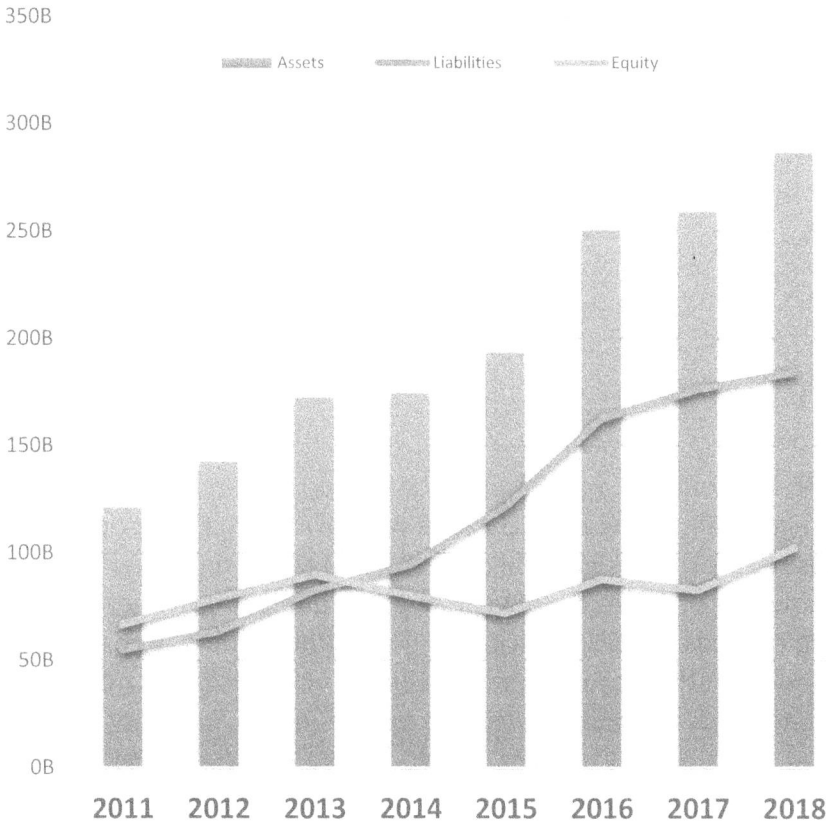

Assets · Liabilities · Equity

2011	2012	2013	2014	2015	2016	2017	2018	

BALANCE SHEET

121,271	142,431	172,384	174,472	193,468	250,312	258,848	286,556	**Assets**
54,908	63,487	82,600	94,389	121,471	162,601	176,130	184,226	**Liabilities**
66,363	78,944	89,784	80,083	71,997	87,711	82,718	102,330	**Equity**
8,506	8,470	8,399	8,254	8,013	7,832	7,794	7,753	**Shares** (diluted)
7.80	9.32	10.69	9.70	8.99	11.20	10.61	13.20	**Book Value** (per share)

MSFT

52

14

NKE

NIKE

NKE was founded in 1967 and is headquartered in Beaverton, Oregon. According to NKE's 2018 Annual Report, their primary business is the design, development, manufacturing and marketing of athletic footwear, apparel, equipment, accessories and related services. Specifically, NKE is the world's largest vendor of athletic footwear and apparel. NKE also owns iconic brands such as Converse, Hurley, and Air Jordan.

NKE has five main sources of revenue. Listed in order from largest percentage of income to least, NKE's revenue segments are, footwear (61.92%), apparel (29.53%), converse (4.87%), equipment (3.59%), and global brands (0.11%). Over 43% of NKE's revenues are earned outside of the United States.

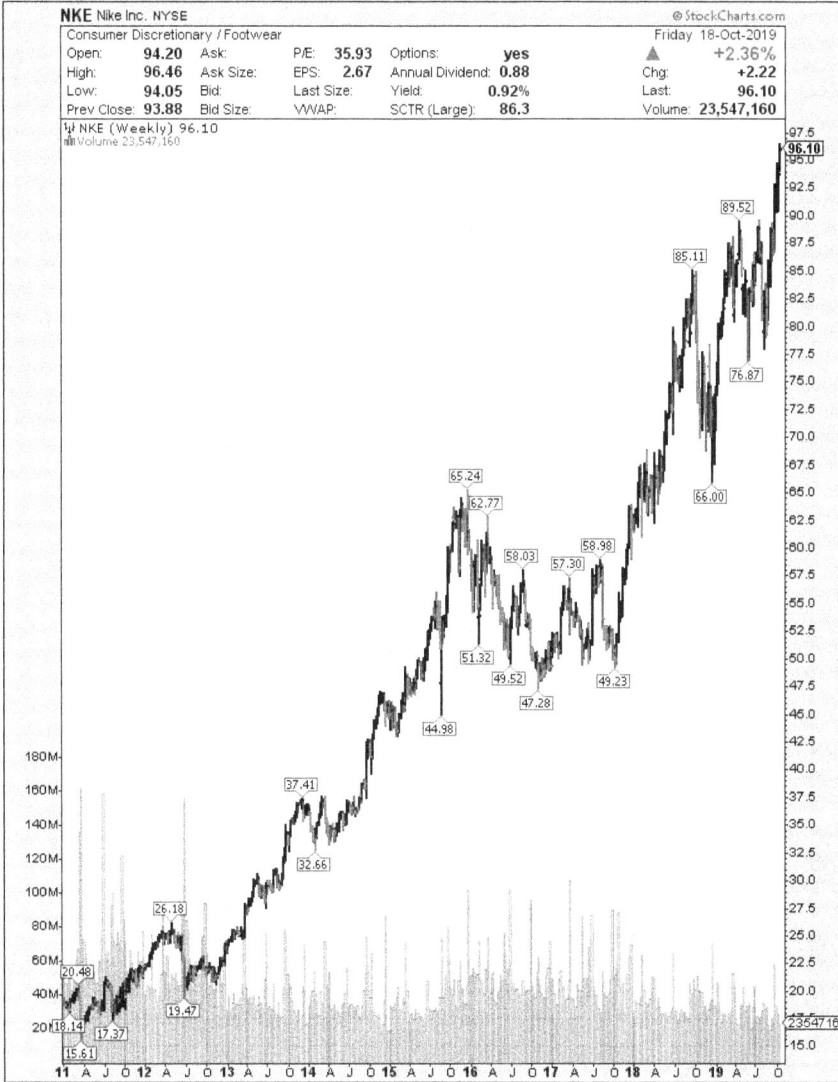

NKE Nike Inc. NYSE						@ StockCharts.com
Consumer Discretionary / Footwear						Friday 18-Oct-2019
Open:	94.20	Ask:	P/E: 35.93	Options:	yes	▲ +2.36%
High:	96.46	Ask Size:	EPS: 2.67	Annual Dividend: 0.88		Chg: +2.22
Low:	94.05	Bid:	Last Size:	Yield: 0.92%		Last: 96.10
Prev Close: 93.88		Bid Size:	VWAP:	SCTR (Large): 86.3		Volume: 23,547,160

NKE stock price chart courtesy of Stockcharts.com

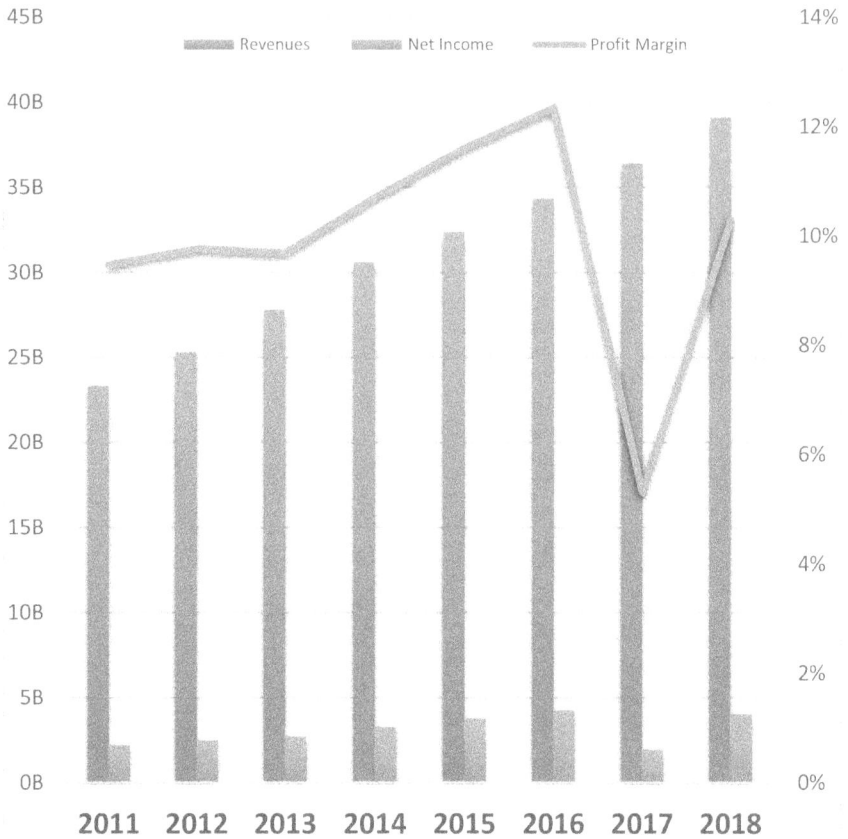

INCOME STATEMENT								
23,331	25,313	27,799	30,601	32,376	34,350	36,397	39,117	**Revenues**
2,211	2,472	2,693	3,273	3,760	4,240	1,933	4,029	**Net Income**
9.48%	9.77%	9.69%	10.70%	11.61%	12.34%	5.31%	10.30%	**Profit Margin**

Stockabet 2019:
An A Through Z Snapshot of 26 Influential Companies

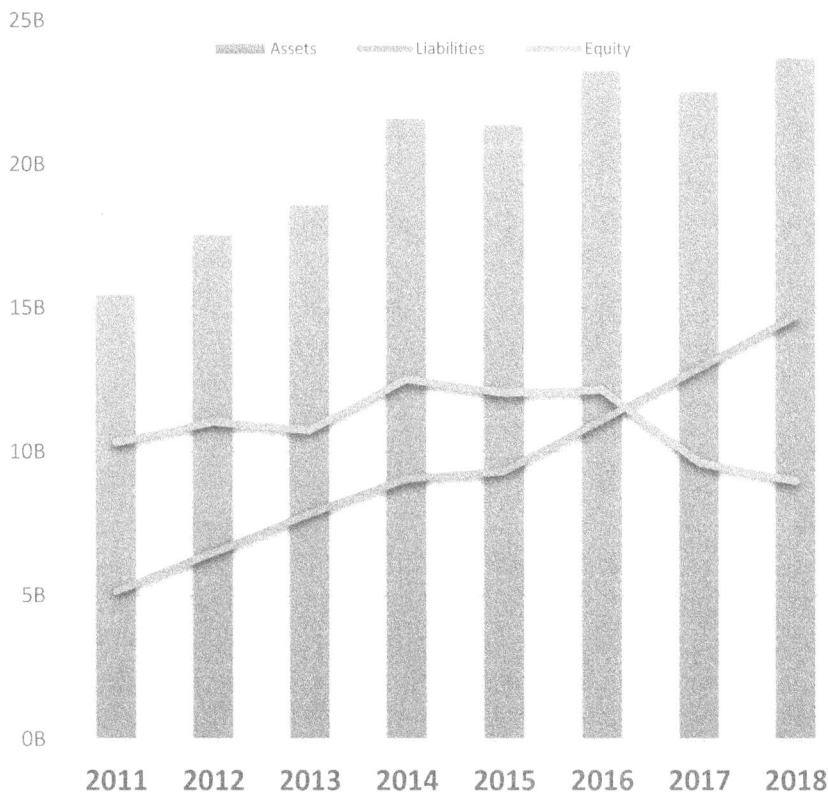

Legend: Assets — Liabilities — Equity

2011	2012	2013	2014	2015	2016	2017	2018	
15,465	17,545	18,594	21,597	21,379	23,259	22,536	23,717	**Assets**
5,139	6,498	7,855	9,065	9,320	11,106	12,914	14,731	**Liabilities**
10,326	11,047	10,739	12,532	12,059	12,153	9,622	8,986	**Equity**
								Shares
940	916	1,812	1,769	1,743	1,692	1,659	1,618	(diluted)
								Book Value
10.99	12.05	5.93	7.09	6.92	7.18	5.80	5.55	(per share)

BALANCE SHEET

NKE

15

OMC

Omnicom Group

OMC was founded in 1986 and is headquartered in New York, New York. According to OMC's 2018 Annual Report, their primary business is providing advertising, marketing and corporate communications services to clients. OMC is a global holding company and is the parent of five main subsidiaries which include BBDO Worldwide, DAS Group, DDB, TBWA Worldwide, and Omnicom Media Group. Each subsidiary is further comprised of several smaller advertising agencies.

OMC has five main sources of revenue. Listed in order from largest percentage of income to least, OMC's revenue segments are, advertising (56.16%), CRM experience (17.14%), CRM execution & support (12.43%), public relations (9.39%), and healthcare (6.89%). Over 44.78% of OMC's revenues are earned outside of the United States.

OmnicomGroup

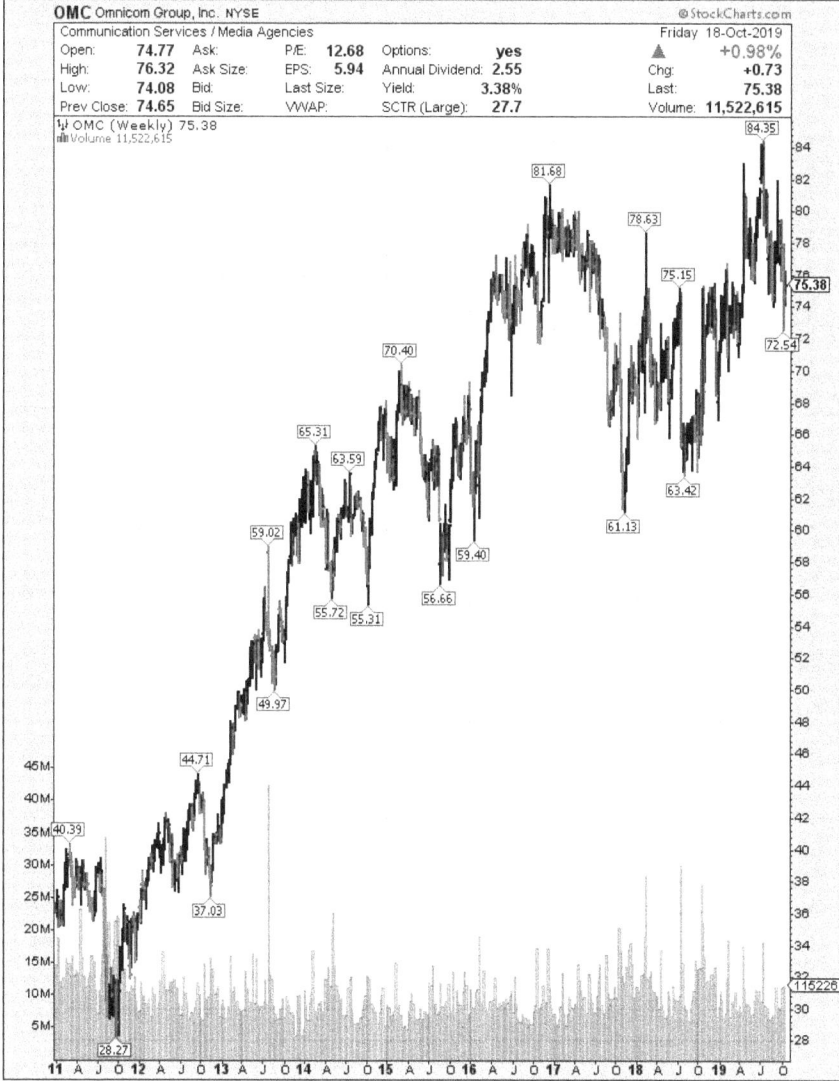

OMC stock price chart courtesy of Stockcharts.com

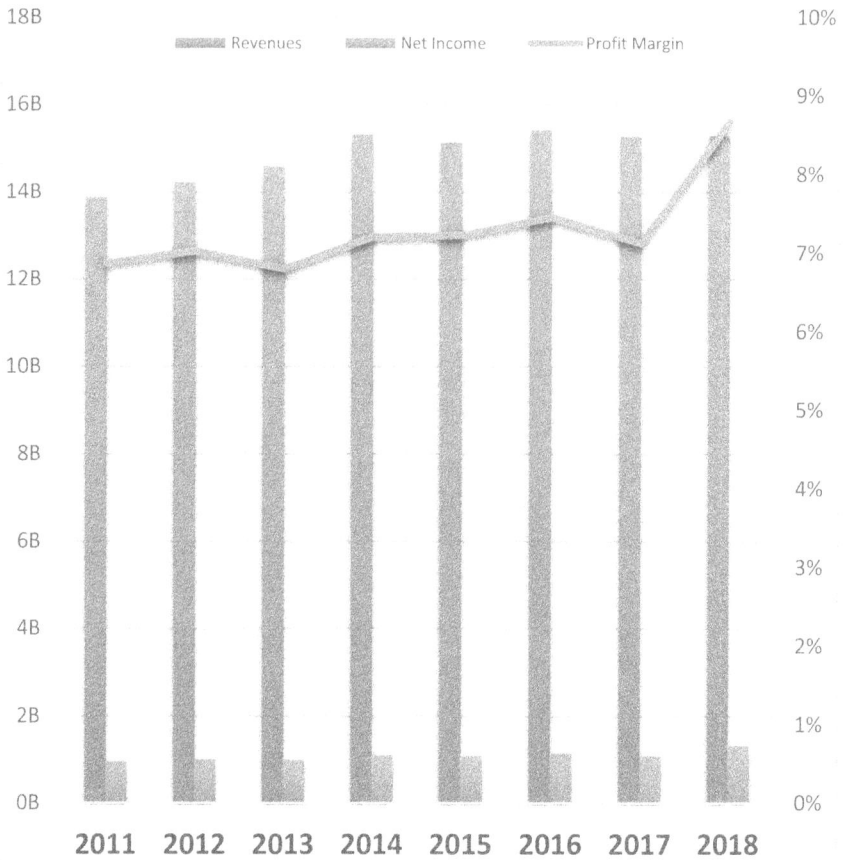

			INCOME	STATEMENT				
13,873	14,219	14,585	15,318	15,134	15,417	15,274	15,290	**Revenues**
953	998	991	1,104	1,094	1,149	1,088	1,326	**Net Income**
6.87%	7.02%	6.80%	7.21%	7.23%	7.45%	7.13%	8.67%	**Profit Margin**

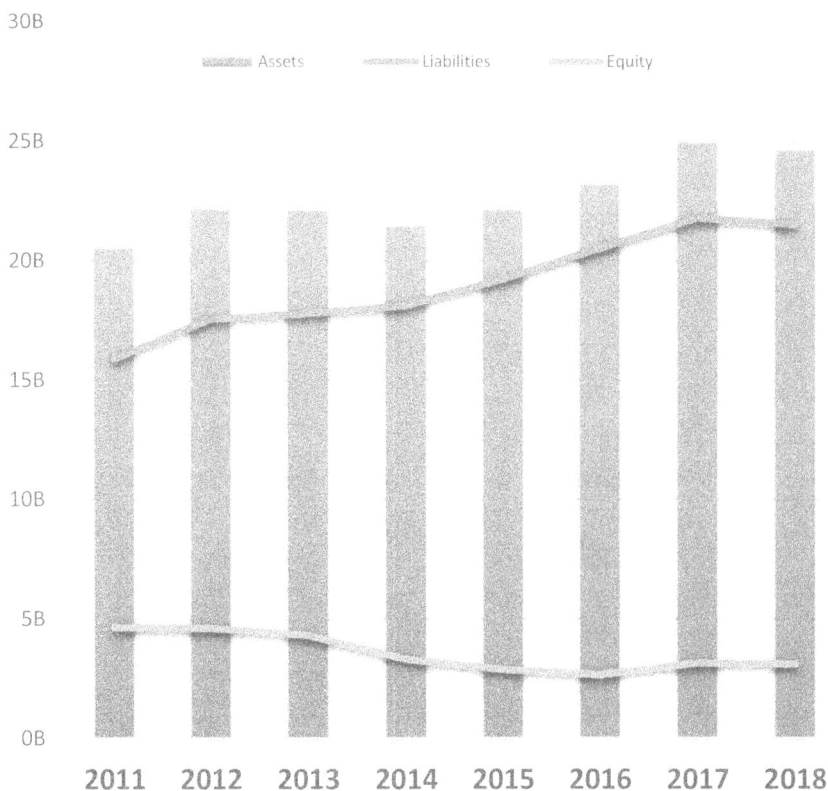

20,505	22,152	22,099	21,428	22,111	23,165	24,931	24,617	**Assets**
15,866	17,536	17,778	18,107	19,221	20,506	21,779	21,510	**Liabilities**
4,639	4,616	4,321	3,321	2,889	2,660	3,152	3,107	**Equity**
								Shares
283	270	260	255	245	239	234	228	(diluted)
								Book Value
16.38	17.10	16.59	13.01	11.78	11.12	13.48	13.65	(per share)

16

PEP

PepsiCo

PEP was founded in 1919 and is headquartered in Purchase, New York. According to PEP's 2018 Annual Report, their primary business is the manufacturing, marketing and distribution of a wide variety of bottled beverages and snacks. Specifically, PEP is leading global food company which owns iconic brands such as Doritos, Gatorade, Tropicana, Quaker Oats, Bubly, Ruffles, Cheetos, Tostitos, 7Up, Mountain Dew, and Sabra.

PEP has six main sources of revenue. Listed in order from largest percentage of income to least, PEP's revenue segments are, North American Beverages (32.59%), Frito-Lay North America (25.28%), Europe Sub-Saharan Africa (17.82%), Latin America (11.37%), Asia Middle East North Africa (9.13%), and Quaker Foods North America (3.81%). Over 47.19% of PEP's revenues are earned outside of the United States.

PEPSICO

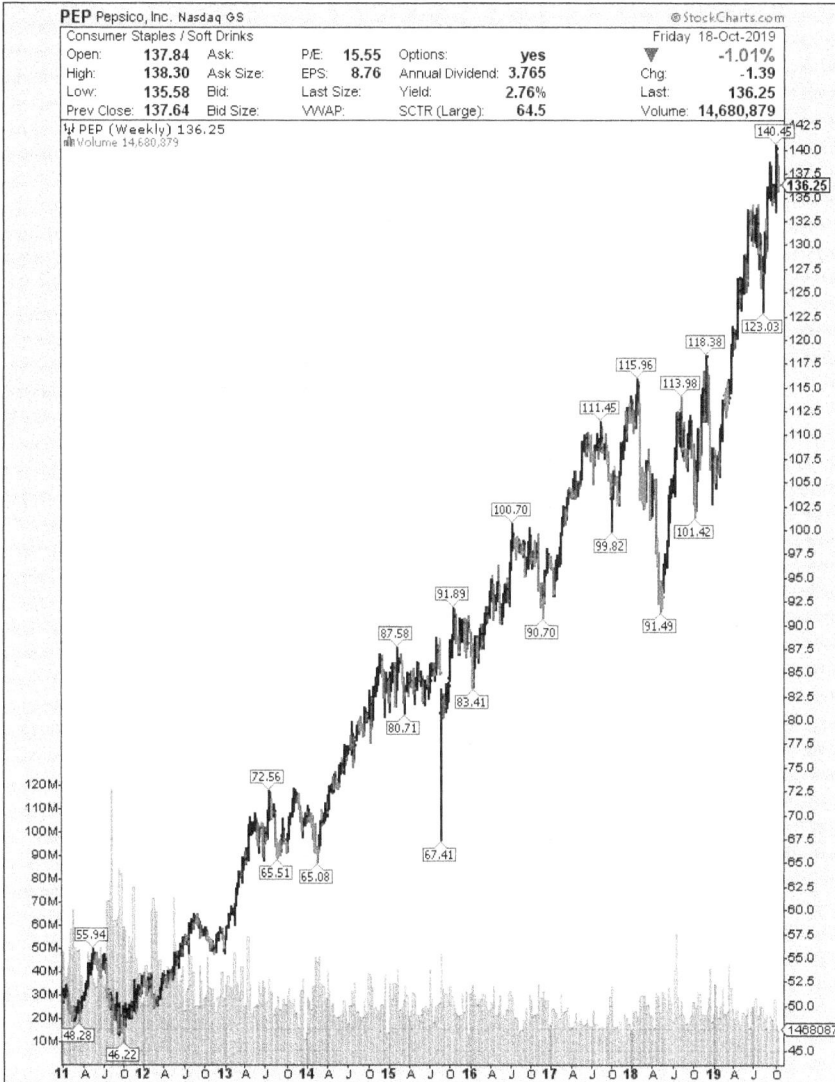

PEP stock price chart courtesy of Stockcharts.com

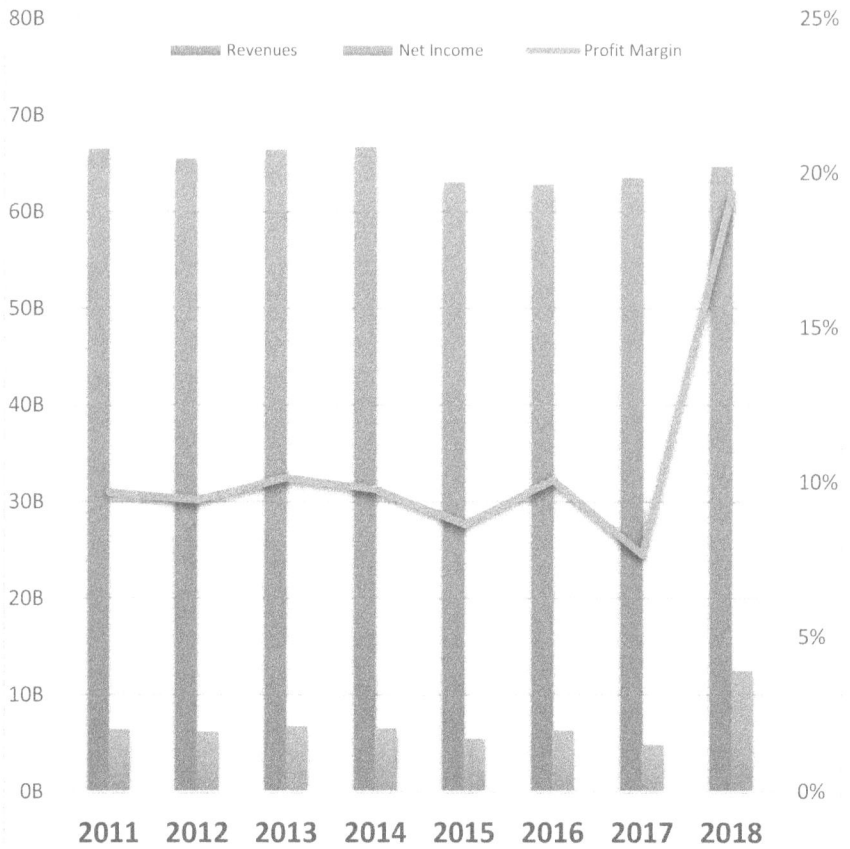

Revenues	Net Income	Profit Margin

2011 2012 2013 2014 2015 2016 2017 2018

INCOME STATEMENT

66,504	65,492	66,415	66,683	63,056	62,799	63,525	64,661	**Revenues**
6,443	6,178	6,740	6,513	5,452	6,329	4,857	12,515	**Net Income**
9.69%	9.43%	10.15%	9.77%	8.65%	10.08%	7.65%	19.35%	**Profit Margin**

PEP

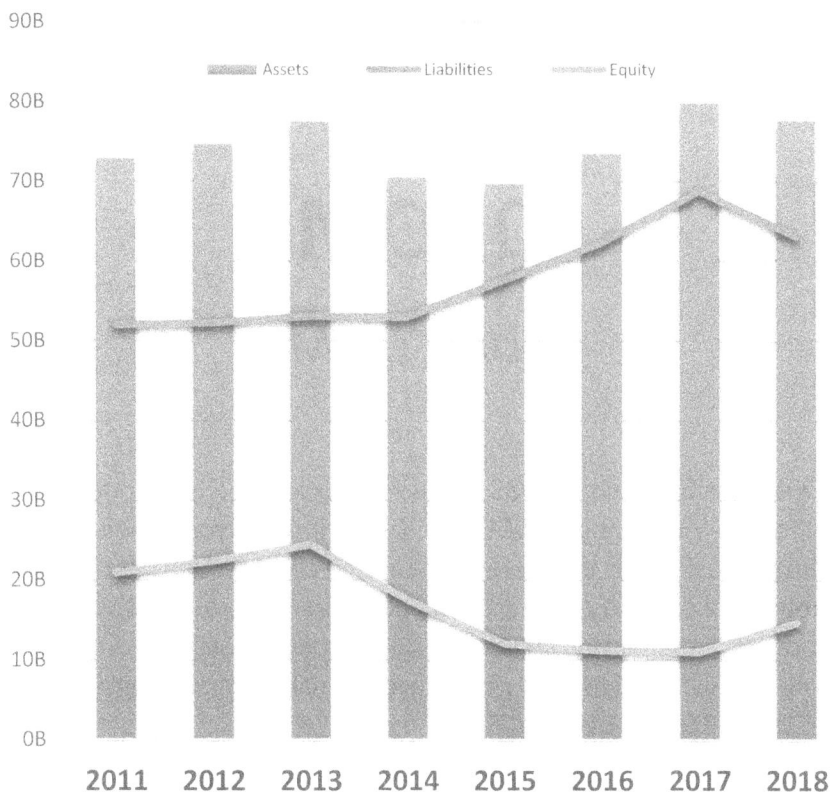

72,882	74,638	77,478	70,509	69,667	73,490	79,804	77,648	**Assets**
51,983	52,239	53,089	52,961	57,637	62,291	68,823	63,046	**Liabilities**
20,899	22,399	24,389	17,548	12,030	11,199	10,981	14,602	**Equity**
								Shares
1,597	1,575	1,560	1,527	1,485	1,452	1,438	1,425	**(diluted)**
								Book Value
13.09	14.22	15.63	11.49	8.10	7.71	7.64	10.25	**(per share)**

BALANCE SHEET

PEP

17

QCOM

QUALCOMM

QCOM was founded in 1985 and is headquartered in San Diego, California. According to QCOM's 2018 Annual Report, their primary business is the development and commercialization of its intellectual property related to its portfolio integrated circuit products. Specifically, QCOM's technology connects billions of mobile devices across the globe through common standards such as CDMA, 3G, 4G, LTE, and 5G.

QOCM has three main sources of revenue. Their largest revenue segment is CDMA Technologies (76.66%), followed by Technology Licensing (22.90%), and finally Strategic Initiatives (0.44%). Over 97.35% of QCOM's revenues are earned outside of the United States, primarily in China and South Korea.

Qualcomm

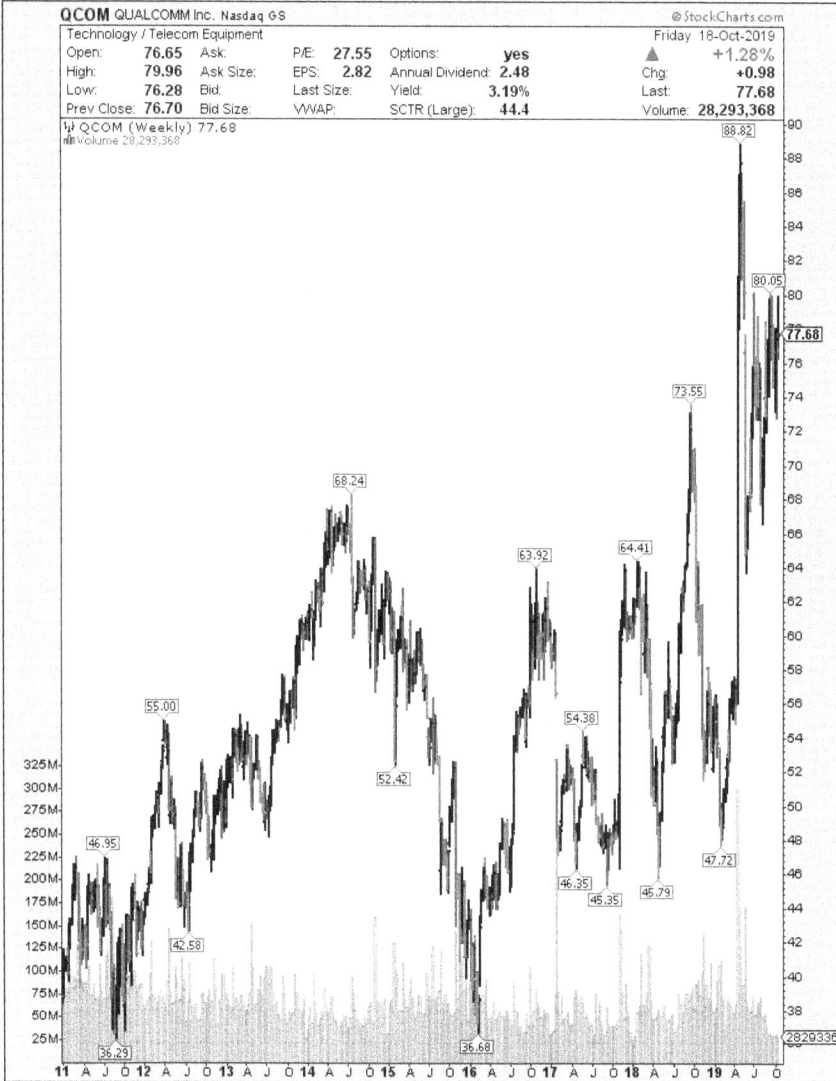

QCOM stock price chart courtesy of Stockcharts.com

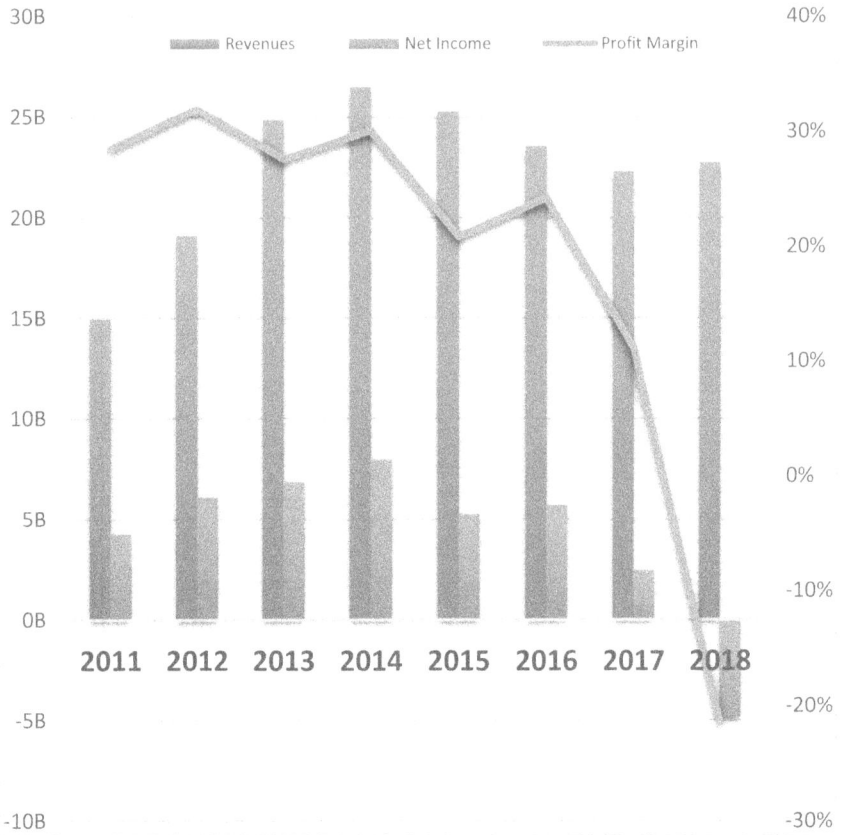

	INCOME	STATEMENT						
14,957	19,121	24,866	26,487	25,281	23,554	22,291	22,732	**Revenues**
4,260	6,109	6,853	7,967	5,271	5,705	2,466	(4,864)	**Net Income**
28.48%	31.95%	27.56%	30.08%	20.85%	24.22%	11.06%	-21.40%	**Profit Margin**

2011 2012 2013 2014 2015 2016 2017 2018 QCOM

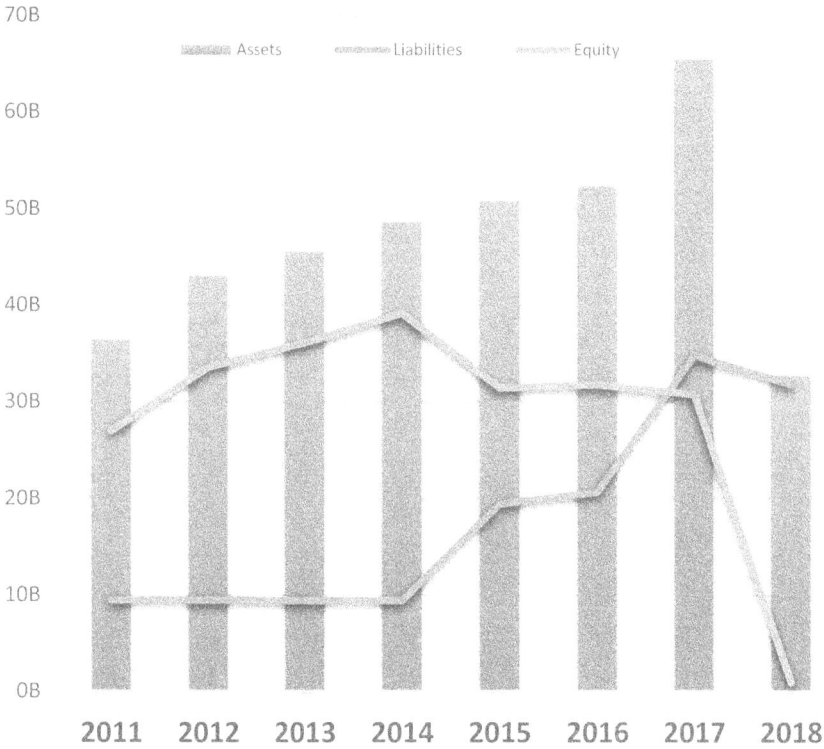

36,422	43,012	45,516	48,574	50,796	52,359	65,486	32,686	**Assets**
9,450	9,467	9,429	9,408	19,382	20,591	34,740	31,758	**Liabilities**
26,972	33,545	36,087	39,166	31,414	31,768	30,746	928	**Equity**
								Shares
1,691	1,741	1,754	1,714	1,639	1,498	1,490	1,463	**(diluted)**
								Book Value
15.95	19.27	20.57	22.85	19.17	21.21	20.63	0.63	**(per share)**

18

RCL

Royal Caribbean Cruises

RCL was founded in 1968 and is headquartered in Miami, Florida. RCL is the second largest cruise and entertainment company in the world. According to RCL's 2018 Annual Report, they operate four cruise brands such as Royal Caribbean International, Celebrity Cruises, Azamara Club Cruises, and Silversea Cruises. RCL also owns majority interests in TUI Cruises based in Germany and Pullmantur Cruises in Spain. Overall RCL operates over 60 cruise ships across the globe with a capacity of 135,530 berths, which is a nautical term meaning beds.

RCL has two main sources of revenue. Their largest revenue segment is passenger tickets sales (71.50%), followed by onboard and other sales (28.50%). Over 39% of RCL's ticket revenues are earned from passengers outside of the United States.

ROYAL CARIBBEAN CRUISES LTD.

RCL stock price chart courtesy of Stockcharts.com

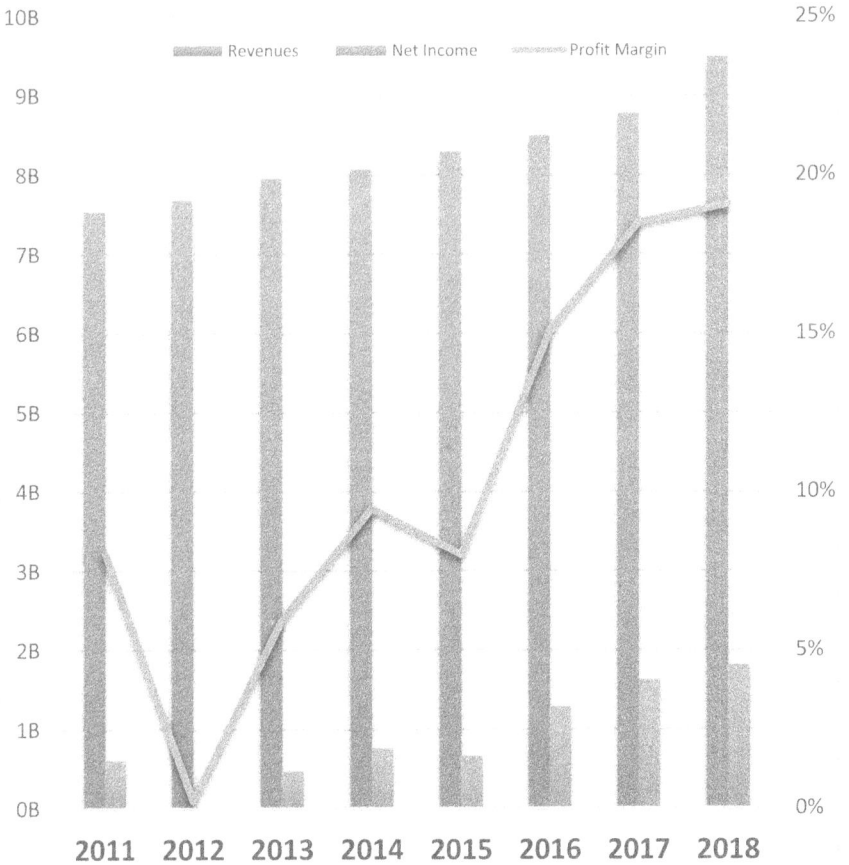

7,537	7,688	7,960	8,074	8,299	8,496	8,778	9,494	**Revenues**
607	18	474	764	666	1,283	1,625	1,811	**Net Income**
8.06%	0.24%	5.95%	9.46%	8.02%	15.11%	18.51%	19.08%	**Profit Margin**

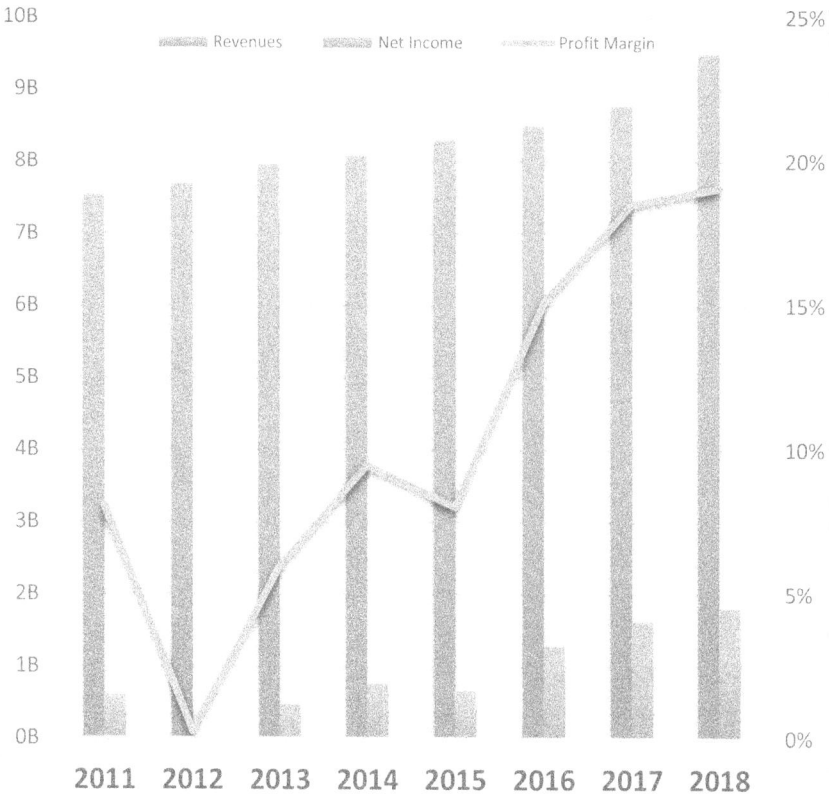

Revenues | Net Income | Profit Margin

	2011	2012	2013	2014	2015	2016	2017	2018

BALANCE SHEET

19,804	19,828	20,073	20,713	20,782	22,310	22,361	27,698	**Assets**
11,481	11,604	11,374	13,900	14,678	13,562	11,659	16,051	**Liabilities**
8,324	8,224	8,699	6,813	6,104	8,748	10,702	11,648	**Equity**
219	220	221	223	221	216	216	212	**Shares** (diluted)
37.97	37.47	39.38	30.55	27.66	40.44	49.62	55.04	**Book Value** (per share)

RCL

19

SBGI

Sinclair Broadcast Group

SBGI was founded in 1986 and is headquartered in Hunt Valley, Maryland. SBGI is a nationally diversified television broadcasting company. According to SBGI's 2018 Annual Report, they own, operate or provide service to 191 television stations which broadcast in aggregate over 605 channels in 89 markets across the United States. SBGI is the largest owner of Fox and ABC network affiliated stations covering an estimated 39% of the United States. Additionally, SBGI owns an investment portfolio commercial and residential real estate.

SBGI has five main sources of revenue. Listed in order from largest percentage of income to least, SBGI's revenue segments are, broadcast advertising (48.58%), broadcast distribution (38.81%), other non-broadcast (6.68%), other non-media (4.46%), and broadcast other (1.46%). SBGI's revenues are earned 100% within the United States.

SINCLAIR

BROADCAST GROUP

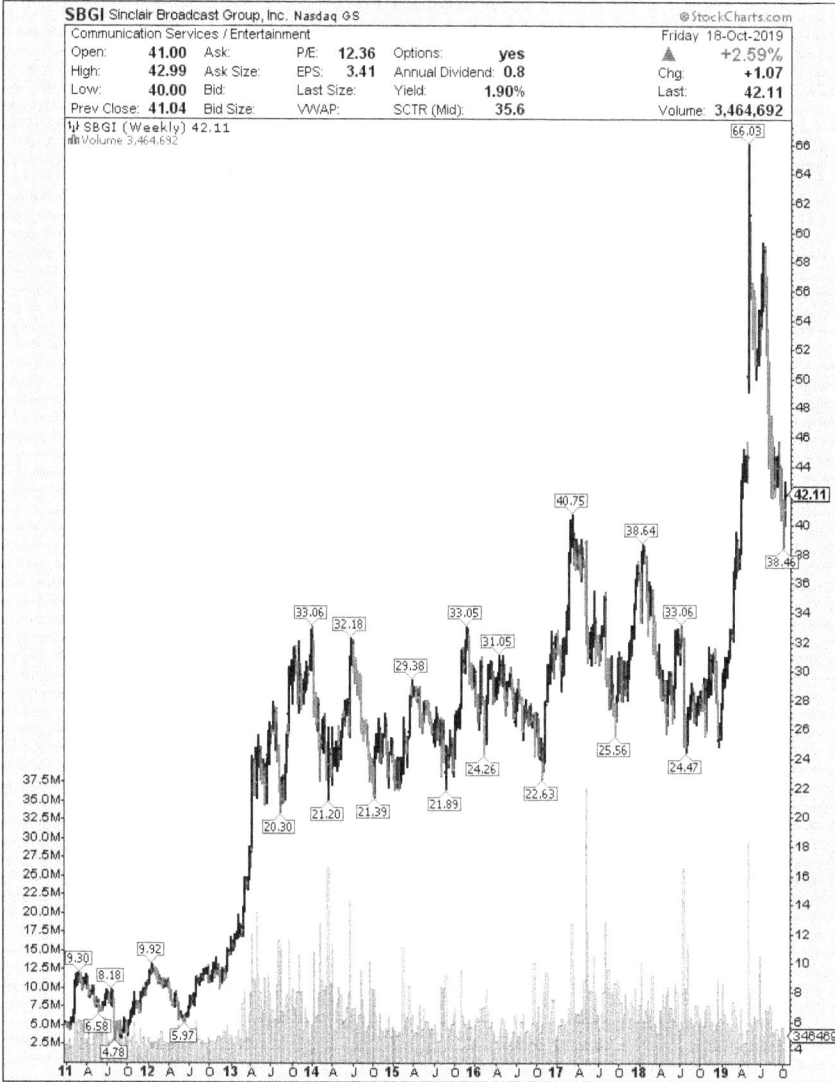

SBGI Sinclair Broadcast Group, Inc. Nasdaq GS						© StockCharts.com
Communication Services / Entertainment						Friday 18-Oct-2019
Open:	41.00	Ask:	P/E:	12.36	Options: yes	▲ +2.59%
High:	42.99	Ask Size:	EPS:	3.41	Annual Dividend: 0.8	Chg: +1.07
Low:	40.00	Bid:	Last Size:		Yield: 1.90%	Last: 42.11
Prev Close: 41.04		Bid Size:	VWAP:		SCTR (Mid): 35.6	Volume: 3,464,692

SBGI stock price chart courtesy of Stockcharts.com

74

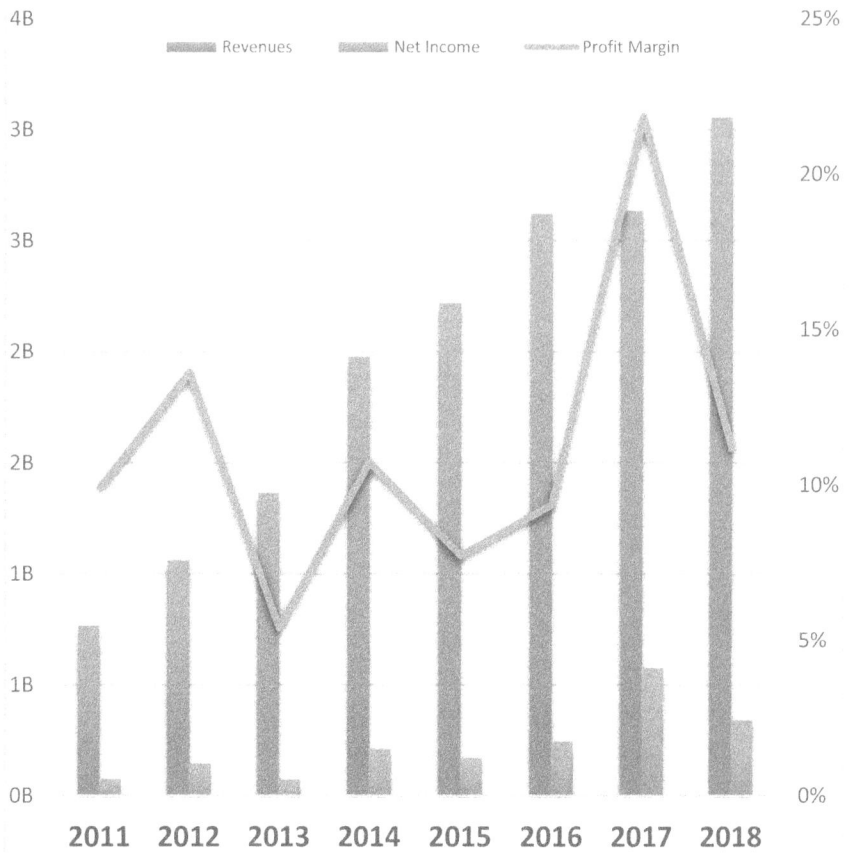

INCOME STATEMENT								
765	1,062	1,363	1,977	2,219	2,623	2,636	3,055	Revenues
76	145	74	212	172	245	576	341	Net Income
9.90%	13.63%	5.39%	10.74%	7.73%	9.35%	21.85%	11.17%	Profit Margin

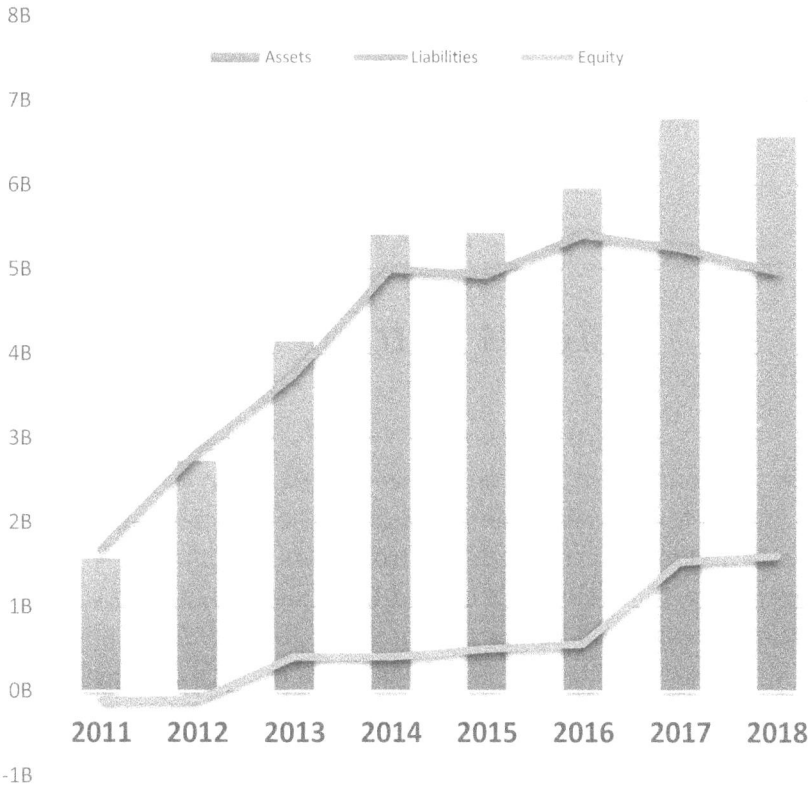

1,571	2,730	4,148	5,410	5,432	5,963	6,785	6,572	**Assets**
1,683	2,830	3,742	5,005	4,933	5,405	5,250	4,972	**Liabilities**
(111)	(100)	406	405	500	558	1,534	1,600	**Equity**
81	81	94	98	96	94	101	102	**Shares (diluted)**
(1.38)	(1.23)	4.33	4.14	5.22	5.91	15.22	15.74	**Book Value (per share)**

SBGI

20

TXN

Texas Instruments

TXN was founded in 1930 and is headquartered in Dallas, Texas. According to TXN's 2018 Annual Report, their primary business is design and manufacturing of electronic semiconductors. Specifically, the technology behind TXN's semiconductors translate real-world signals such as sound, temperature, pressure or images by conditioning, amplifying, and then converting them into digital data. Additionally, TXN produces a variety of graphing calculators such as the iconic TI-83, as well as the TI-84, and TI-89.

TXN has three main sources of revenue. Their largest revenue segment is analog (68.43%), followed by embedded processors (22.52%), and other (9.05%). Over 85.50% of TXN's revenues are earned outside of the United States.

TEXAS INSTRUMENTS

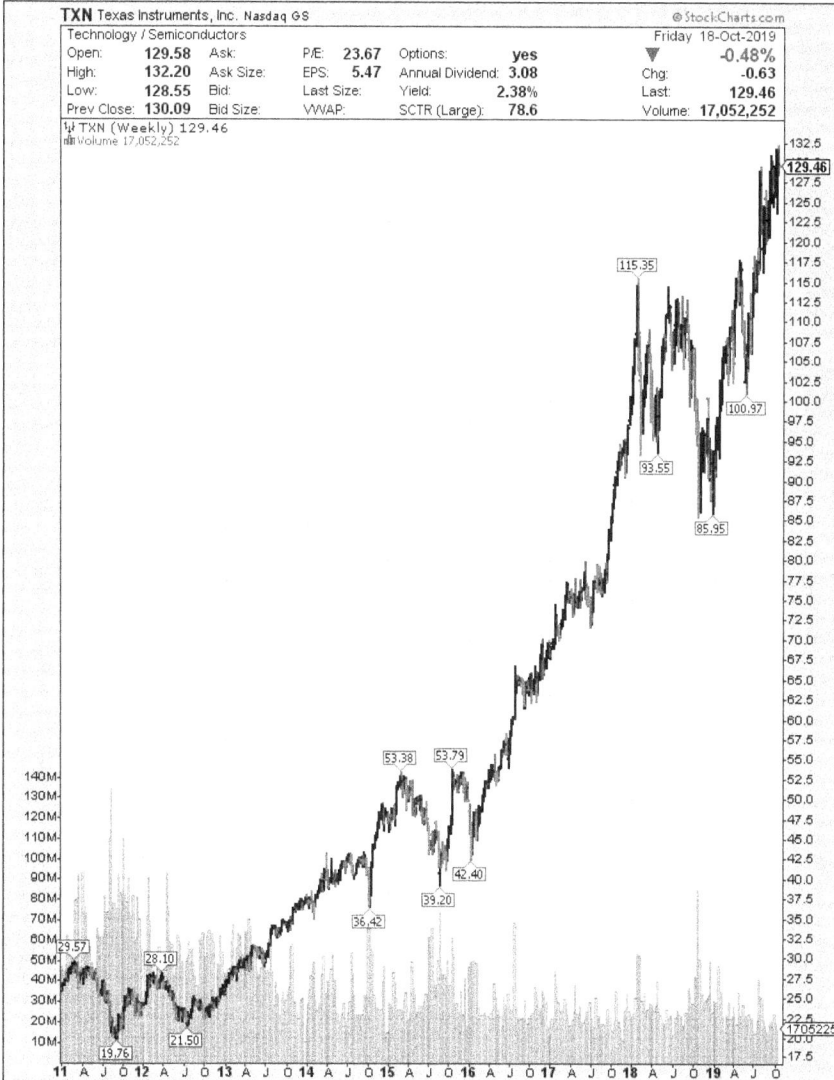

TXN stock price chart courtesy of Stockcharts.com

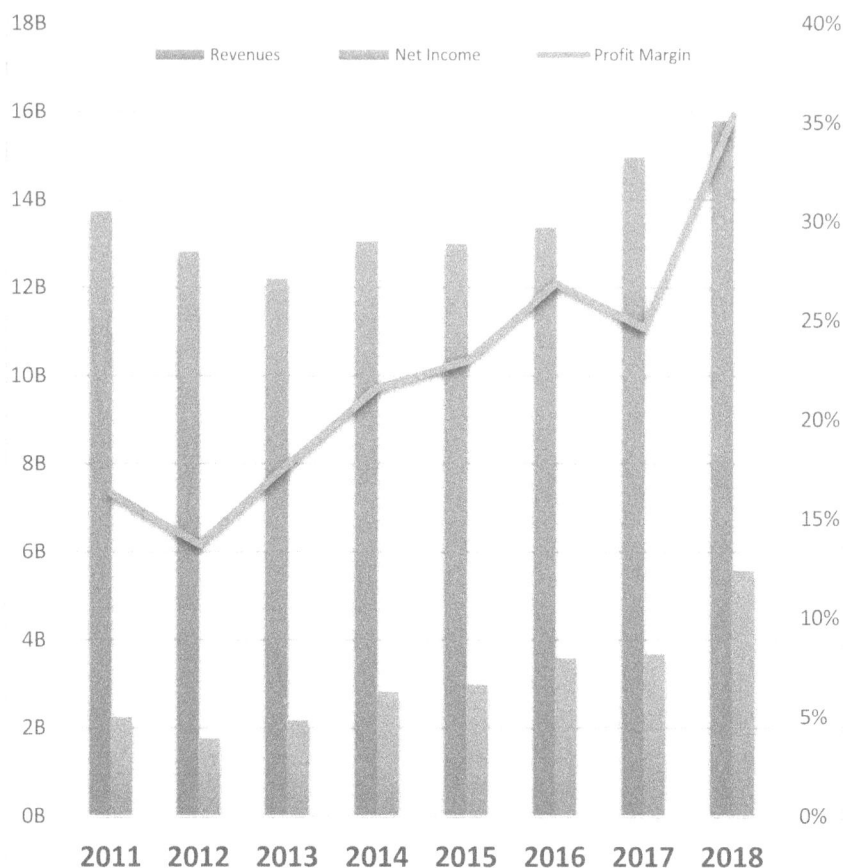

INCOME STATEMENT								
13,735	12,825	12,205	13,045	13,000	13,370	14,961	15,784	**Revenues**
2,236	1,759	2,162	2,821	2,986	3,595	3,682	5,580	**Net Income**
16.28%	13.72%	17.71%	21.63%	22.97%	26.89%	24.61%	35.35%	**Profit Margin**

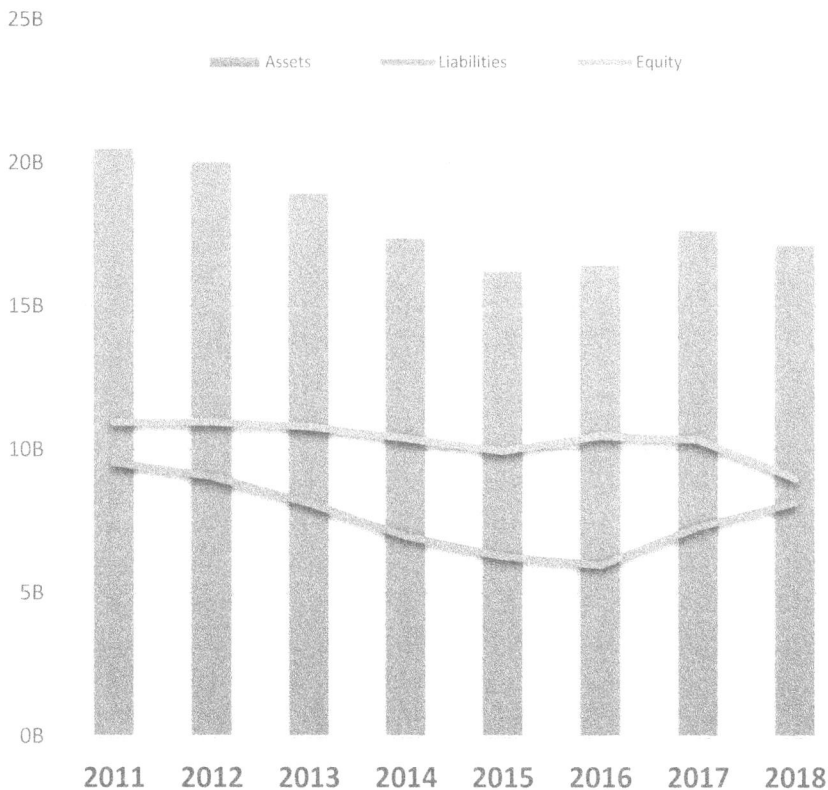

2011	2012	2013	2014	2015	2016	2017	2018	BALANCE SHEET
20,497	20,021	18,938	17,372	16,230	16,431	17,642	17,137	**Assets**
9,545	9,060	8,131	6,982	6,284	5,958	7,305	8,143	**Liabilities**
10,952	10,961	10,807	10,390	9,946	10,473	10,337	8,994	**Equity**
1,171	1,146	1,113	1,080	1,043	1,021	1,012	990	**Shares** (diluted)
9.35	9.56	9.71	9.62	9.54	10.26	10.21	9.08	**Book Value** (per share)

TXN

21

UFPI

Universal Forest Products

UFPI was founded in 1955 and is headquartered in Grand Rapids, Michigan. UFPI is a global lumber holding company comprised of over 77 subsidiaries in the United States, Mexico, Europe, Asia, and Australia. According to UFPI's 2018 Annual Report, their primary business is design, manufacturing, and marketing of wood, engineered wood components, and wood-alternative products. Specifically, UFPI produces pallets, crates, boxes, roof trusses, plywood, composite decking and wood flooring, under such brands as Deckorators, ProWood, and Outdoor Essentials.

UFPIP has three main sources of revenue. Their largest revenue segment is retail (36.42%), followed by industrial (34.10%), and construction (29.48%). Over 12.98% of UFPI's revenues are earned outside of the United States.

Universal Forest Products

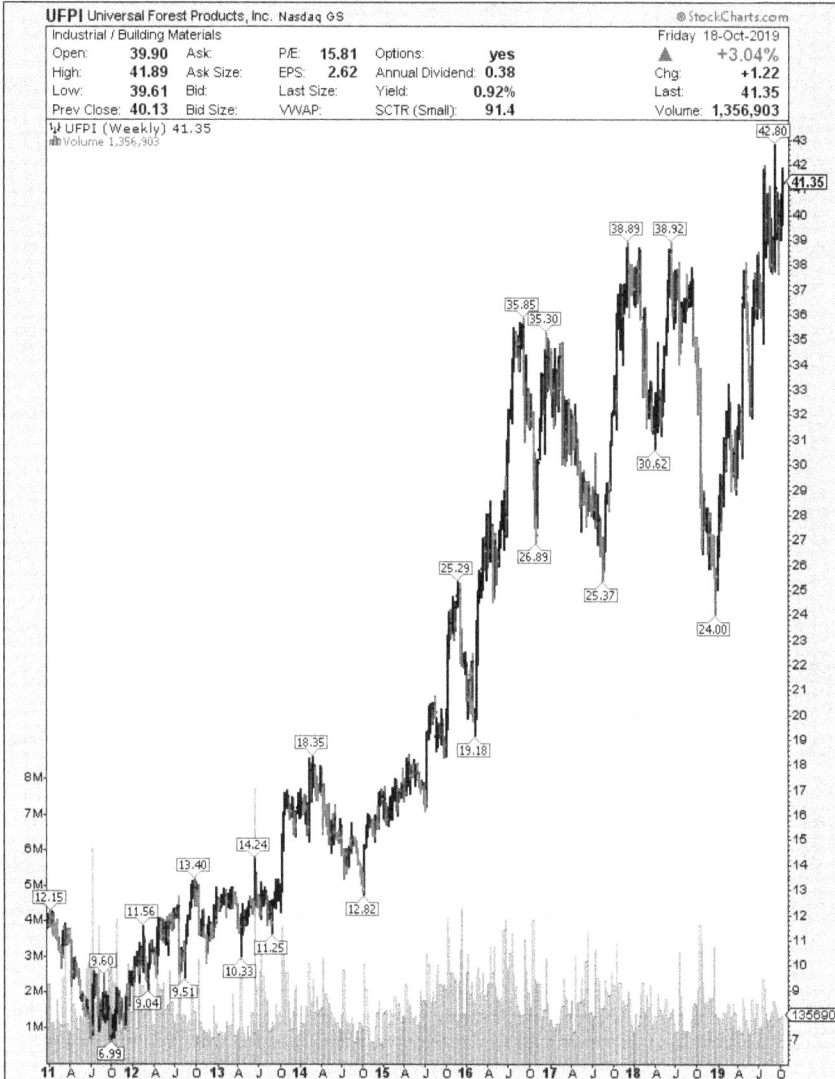

UFPI stock price chart courtesy of Stockcharts.com

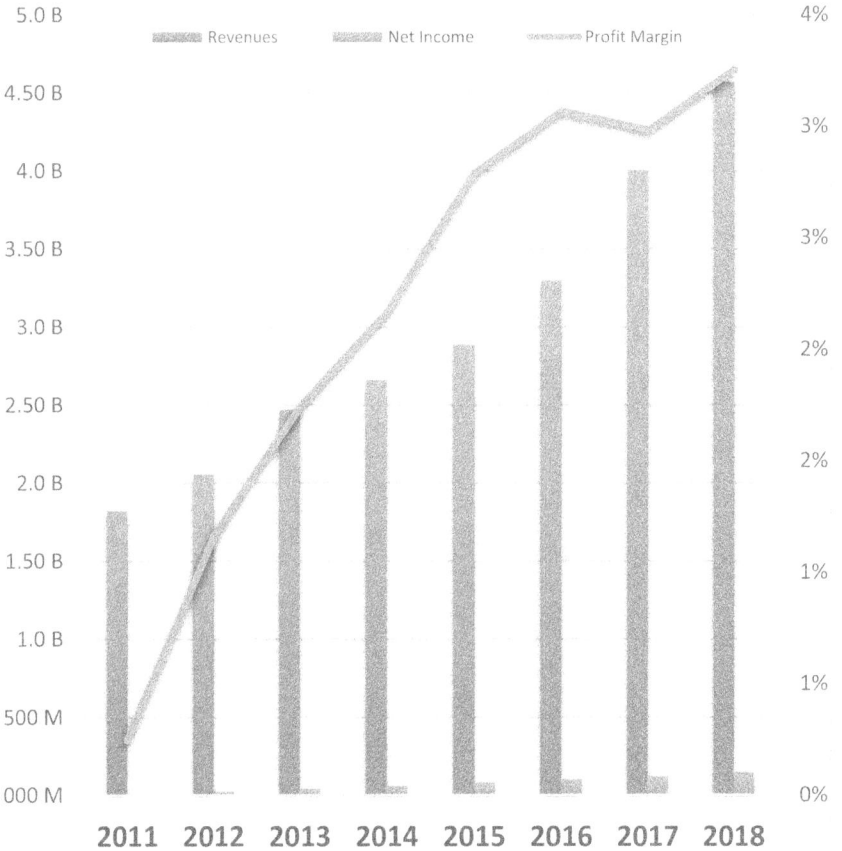

			INCOME	STATEMENT				
1,822	2,055	2,470	2,660	2,887	3,297	4,006	4,566	**Revenues**
5	24	43	58	81	101	120	149	**Net Income**
0.25%	1.16%	1.74%	2.17%	2.79%	3.07%	2.98%	3.25%	**Profit Margin**

Stockabet 2019:
An A Through Z Snapshot of 26 Influential Companies

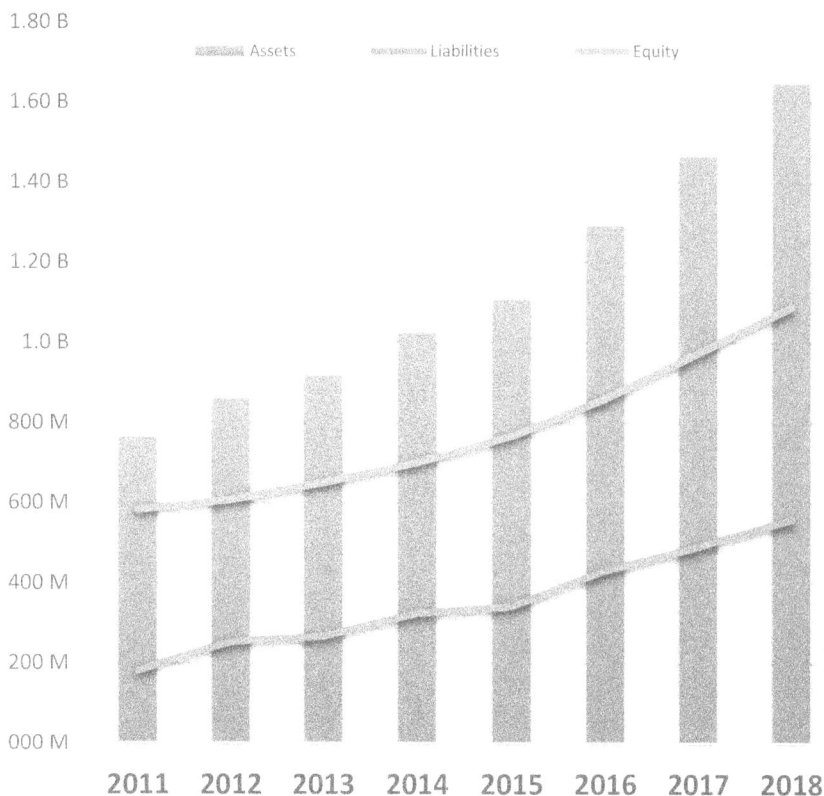

764	861	917	1,024	1,108	1,292	1,465	1,648	**Assets**
181	253	267	324	341	432	491	559	**Liabilities**
583	608	650	700	766	861	974	1,089	**Equity**
								Shares
20	20	20	20	60	60	60	60	(diluted)
								Book Value
29.88	30.99	32.81	35.16	12.79	14.29	16.13	18.02	(per share)

22

VZ

Verizon Communications

VZ was founded in 1983 and is headquartered in New York, New York. VZ is one of the world's leading providers of communications, information and entertainment products and services. According to VZ's 2018 Annual Report, their primary business is developing and operating wireless and wireline communications networks that deliver voice and data services to customers. Additionally, VZ also owns several advertising and media properties such as RYOT, Yahoo!, TechCrunch, Engadget, AOL, Huffpost, Makers, and AutoBlog.

VZ has three main sources of revenue. Their largest revenue segment is wireless (70.10%), followed by wireline (22.74%), and other (8.36%). Only 2.29% of VZ's revenues are earned outside of the United States. This is primarily attributable to VZ's international subsidiary Global IP, which owns and operates an 800,000 mile long fiber optic network in over 150 countries.

verizon✓

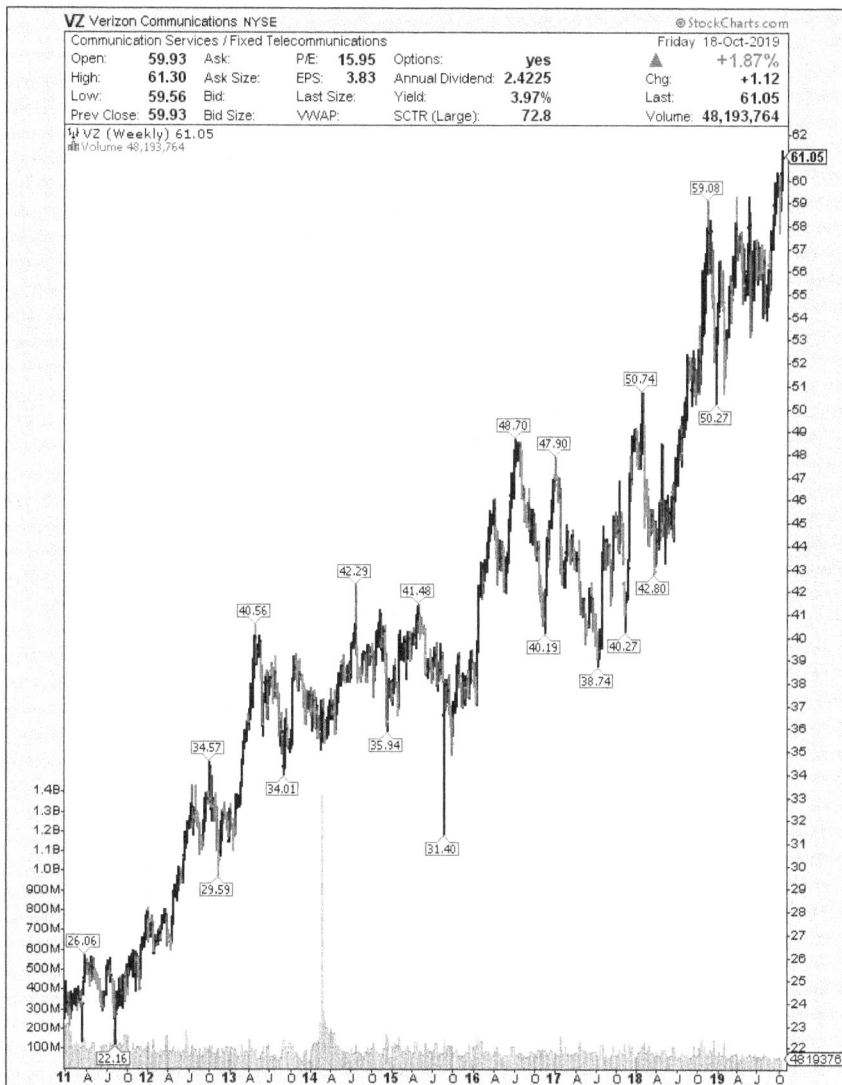

VZ stock price chart courtesy of Stockcharts.com

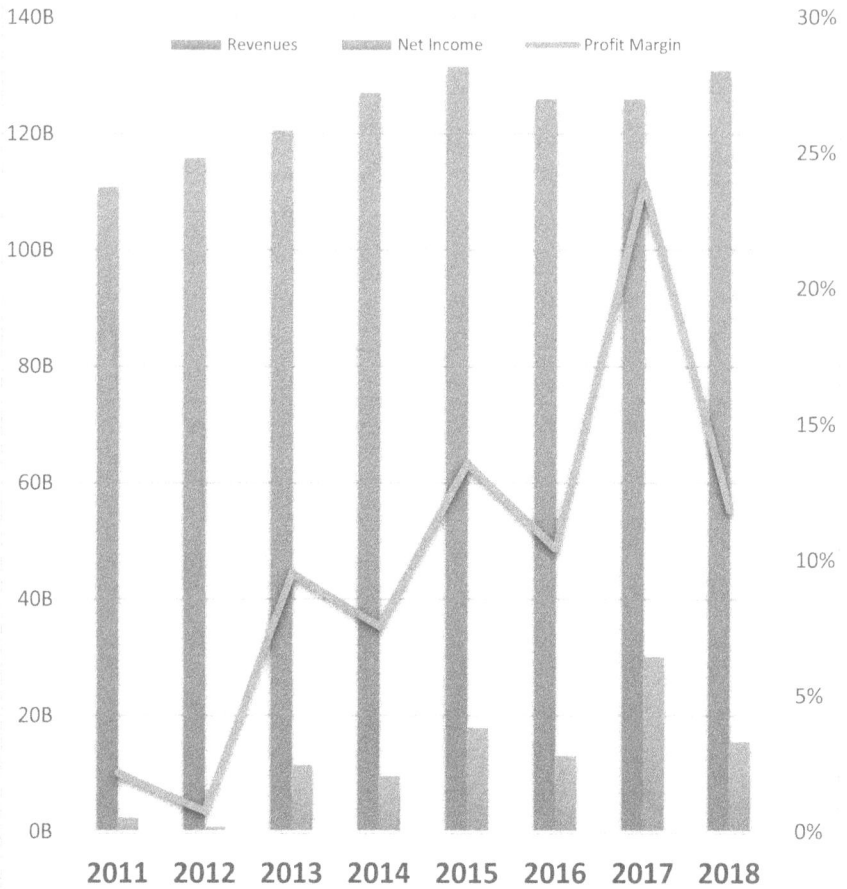

INCOME STATEMENT								
110,875	115,846	120,550	127,079	131,620	125,980	126,034	130,863	**Revenues**
2,404	875	11,497	9,625	17,879	13,127	30,101	15,528	**Net Income**
2.17%	0.76%	9.54%	7.57%	13.58%	10.42%	23.88%	11.87%	**Profit Margin**

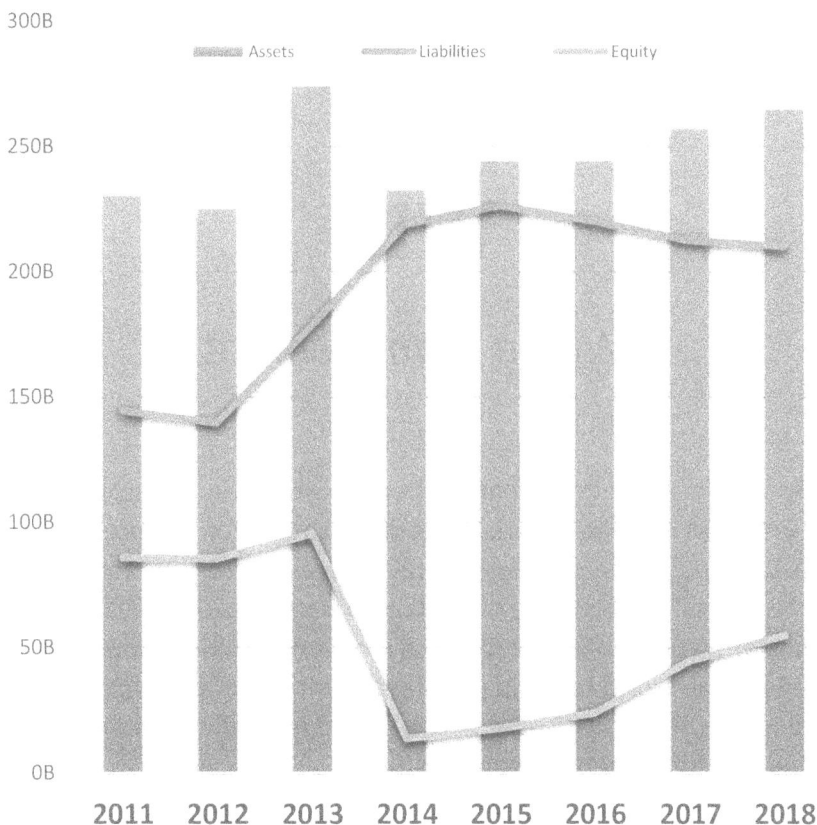

			BALANCE	SHEET				
230,461	225,222	274,098	232,616	244,175	244,180	257,143	264,829	Assets
144,553	139,689	178,682	218,940	226,333	220,148	212,456	210,119	Liabilities
85,908	85,533	95,416	13,676	17,842	24,032	44,687	54,710	Equity
								Shares
2,839	2,862	2,874	3,981	4,093	4,086	4,089	4,132	(diluted)
								Book Value
30.26	29.89	33.20	3.44	4.36	5.88	10.93	13.24	(per share)

VZ

23

WM

Waste Management

WM was founded in 1987 and is headquartered in Houston, Texas. WM is North America's leading provider of comprehensive waste management environmental services. According to WM's 2018 Annual Report, they owned or operated 252 landfills, 312 transfer stations, and 102 material recovery facilities. Specifically, WM partners with municipalities and commercial customers to collect, mange, and dispose of waste. Additionally, WM owns several landfill gas-to-energy facilities.

WM has two main sources of revenue. Their largest revenue segment is solid waste (84.63%), followed by other (15.37%). Only 5.01% of WM's revenues are earned outside of the United States. This is primarily attributable to WM's Canadian subsidiary.

WM

WASTE MANAGEMENT

WM stock price chart courtesy of Stockcharts.com

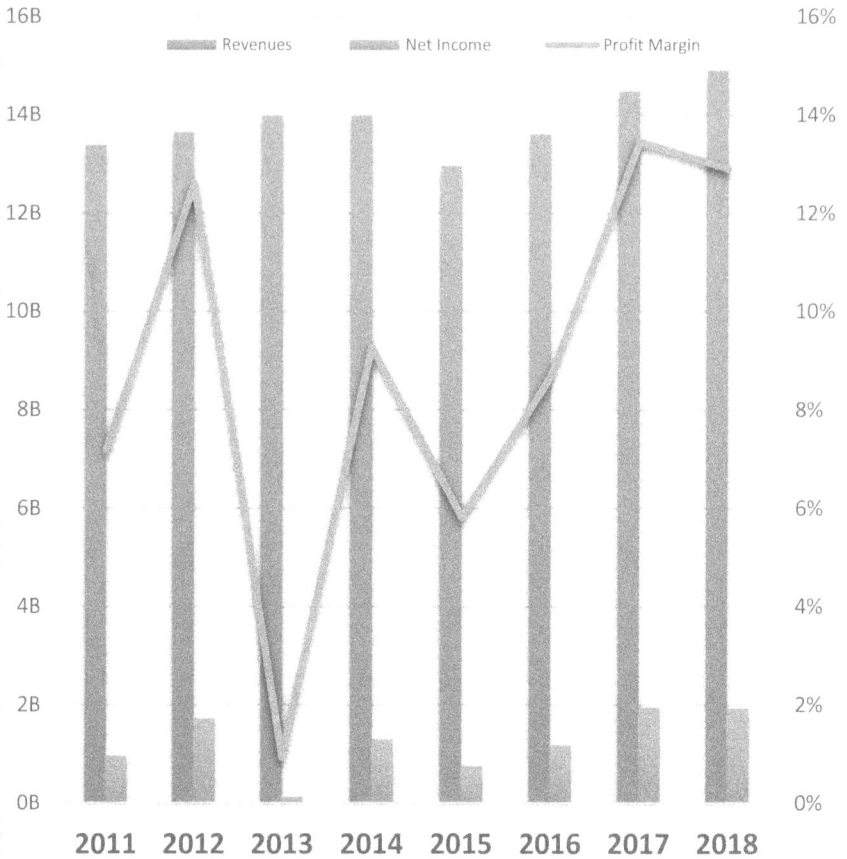

13,378	13,649	13,983	13,996	12,961	13,609	14,485	14,914	**Revenues**
961	1,720	130	1,298	753	1,182	1,949	1,925	**Net Income**
7.18%	12.60%	0.93%	9.27%	5.81%	8.69%	13.46%	12.91%	**Profit Margin**

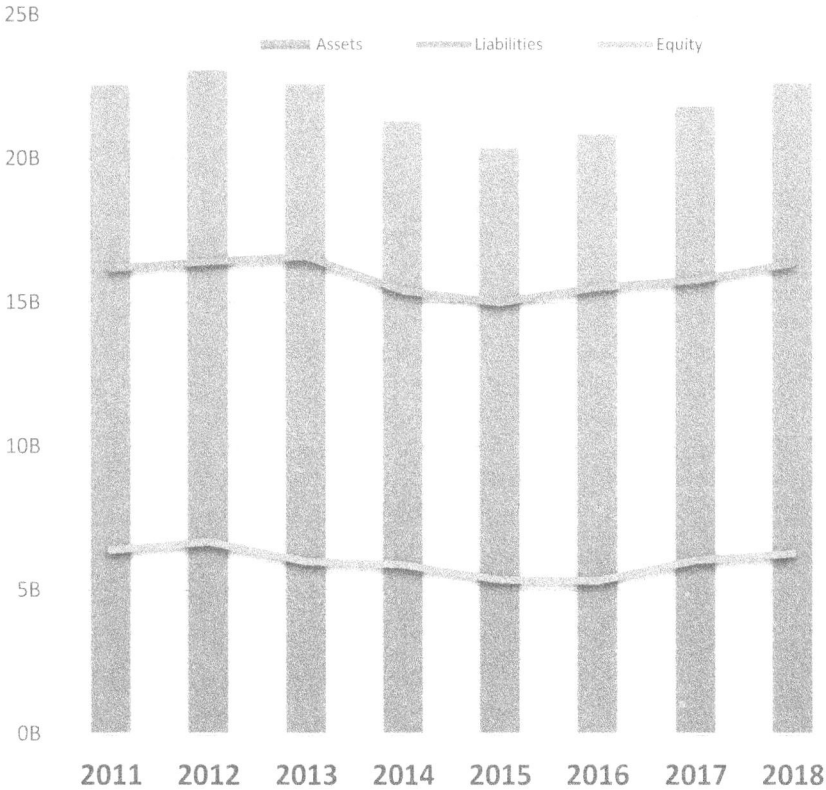

22,569	23,097	22,603	21,297	20,367	20,859	21,829	22,650	**Assets**
16,179	16,422	16,601	15,408	15,000	15,539	15,787	16,374	**Liabilities**
6,390	6,675	6,002	5,889	5,367	5,320	6,042	6,276	**Equity**
471	464	470	466	456	447	442	432	**Shares** (diluted)
13.57	14.39	12.77	12.64	11.77	11.90	13.67	14.53	**Book Value** (per share)

24

XRX

Xerox Holdings

XRX was founded in 1906 and is headquartered in Norwalk, Connecticut. XRX is a print technology and intelligent work solutions provider that owns over 10,307 U.S. design and utility patents related to printing and copying. According to XRX's 2018 Annual Report, their primary business is development and manufacturing of document imaging and printing technology. Specifically, XRX produces copiers and offers a wide variety of associated services such as equipment rentals, maintenance, supplies, and managed document services.

XRX has two main sources of revenue. Their largest revenue segment is post sale services (77.62%), followed by equipment sales (22.38%). Over 39.85% of XRX's revenues are earned outside of the United States. As of January 2020, XRX was pursuing a pending merger with Hewlett-Packard, commonly referred to as HP, Inc.

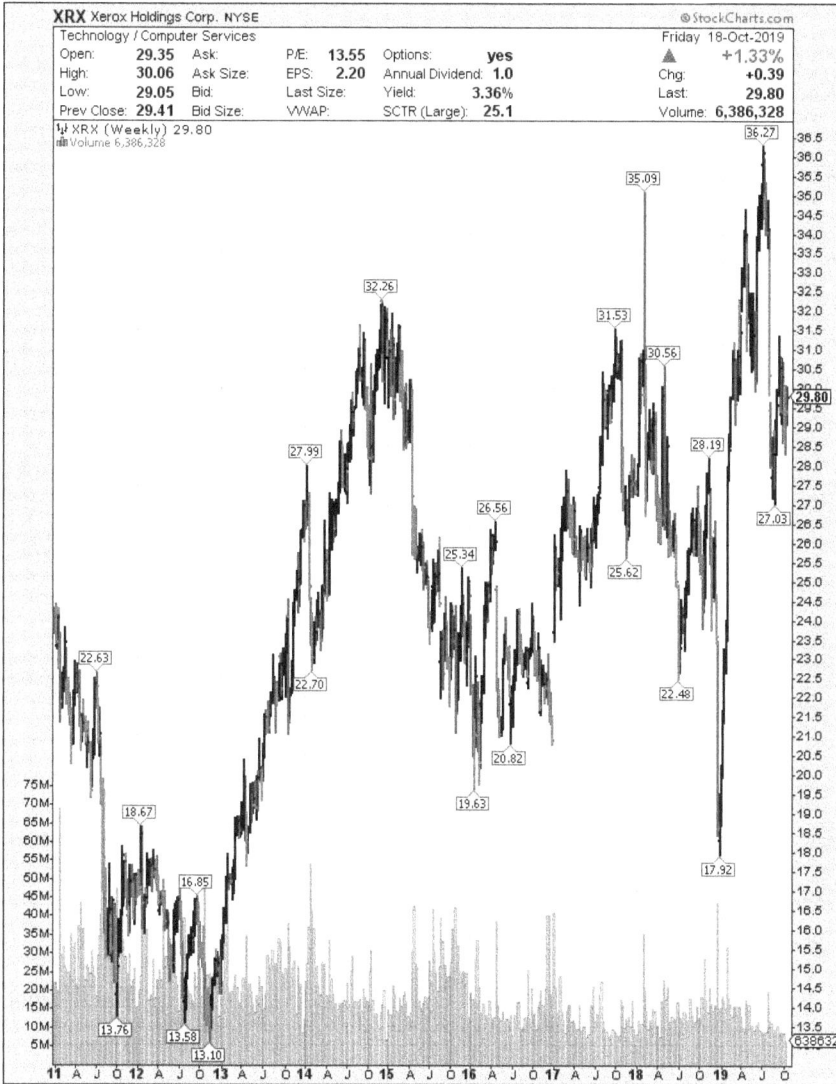

XRX stock price chart courtesy of Stockcharts.com

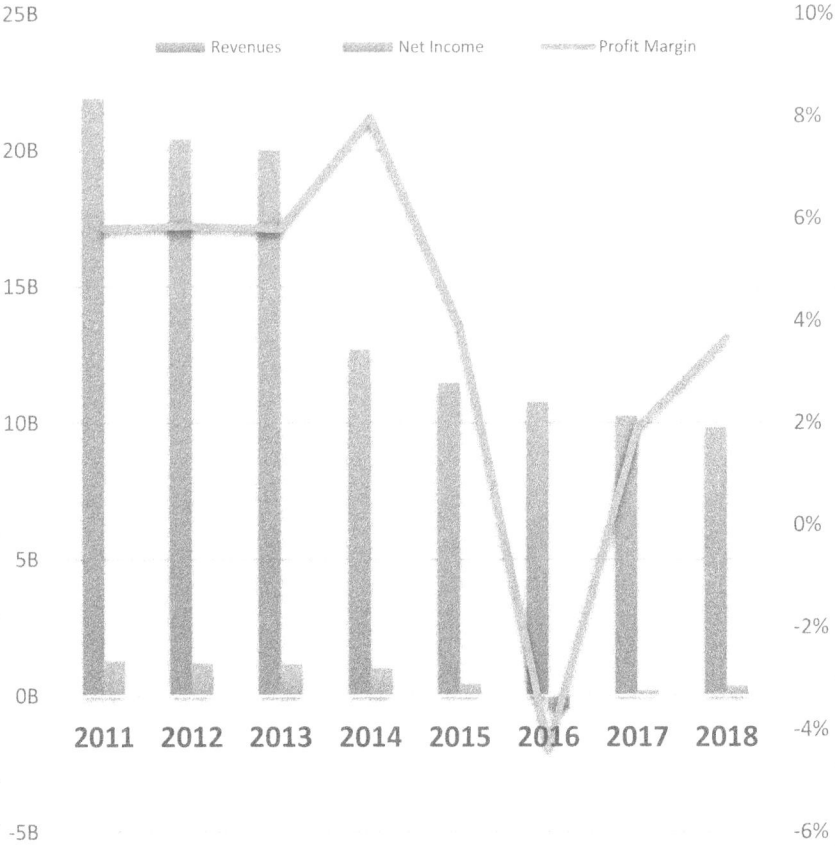

			INCOME		STATEMENT			
21,900	20,421	20,006	12,679	11,465	10,771	10,265	9,830	**Revenues**
1,274	1,195	1,159	1,013	448	(471)	195	361	**Net Income**
5.82%	5.85%	5.79%	7.99%	3.91%	-4.37%	1.90%	3.67%	**Profit Margin**

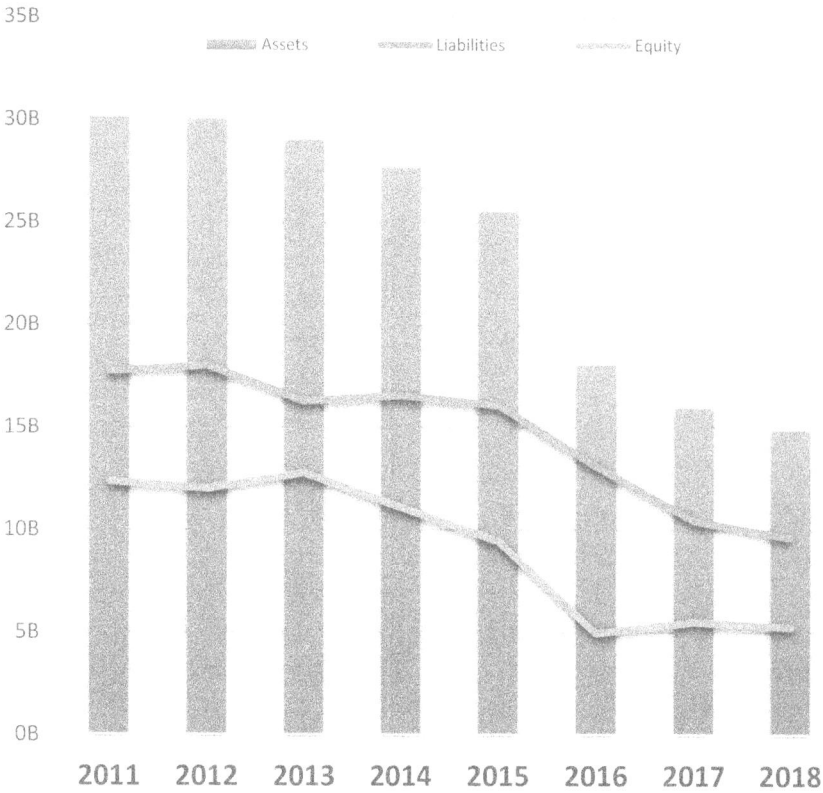

30,116	30,015	29,036	27,658	25,541	18,051	15,946	14,874	**Assets**
17,742	18,002	16,268	16,556	16,075	13,090	10,439	9,621	**Liabilities**
12,374	12,013	12,768	11,102	9,466	4,961	5,507	5,253	**Equity**
								Shares
1,444	1,329	1,274	1,172	1,076	1,024	257	252	**(diluted)**
								Book Value
8.57	9.04	10.03	9.48	8.80	4.84	21.46	20.87	**(per share)**

25

YELP

Yelp

YELP was founded in 2004 and is headquartered in San Francisco, California. YELP aims to connect consumers with local businesses through its trusted online platform. According to YELP's 2018 Annual Report, their primary business is the development and operation of their website and mobile application through the sale of associated advertising. Additionally, YELP offers gift certificates, reservations and the ability for customers to transact directly with businesses through their platform.

YELP has three main sources of revenue. Their largest revenue segment is advertising (96.26%), followed by other (2.29%), and transactions (1.45%). Only 1.40% of YELP's revenues are earned outside of the United States. This is primarily attributable to YELP winding down international sales activities in markets outside of the U.S. and Canada in the fourth quarter of 2016.

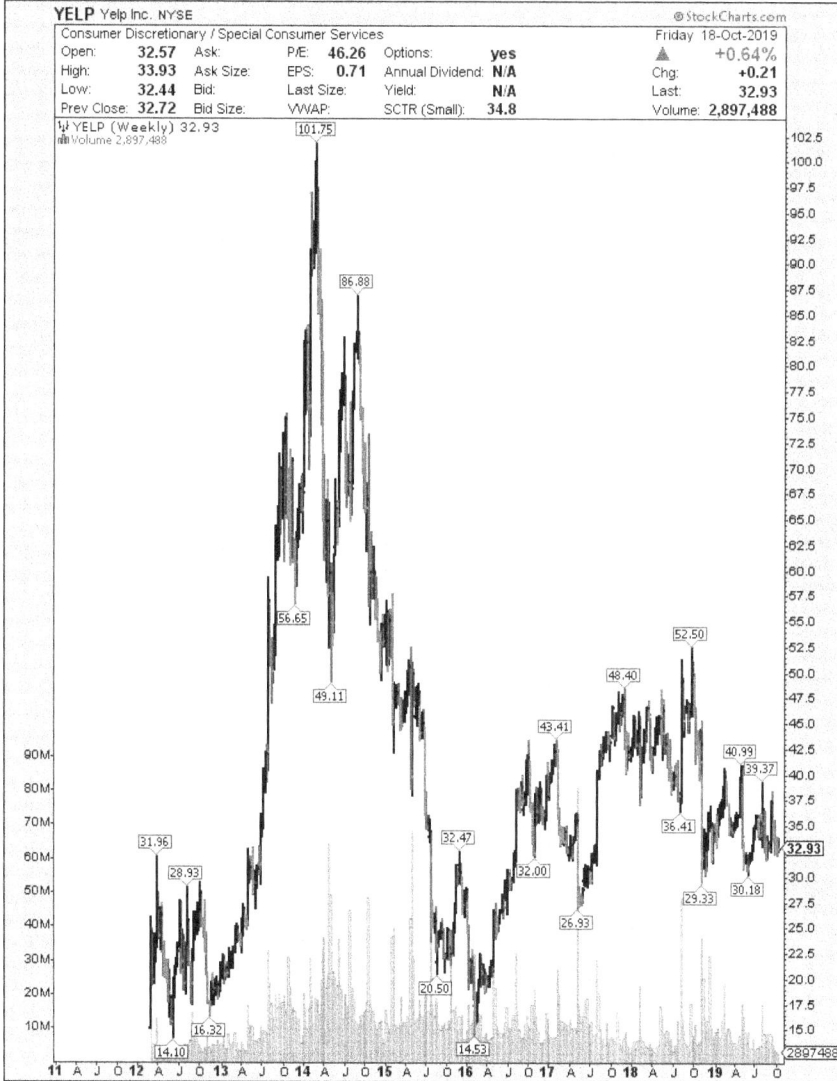

YELP stock price chart courtesy of Stockcharts.com

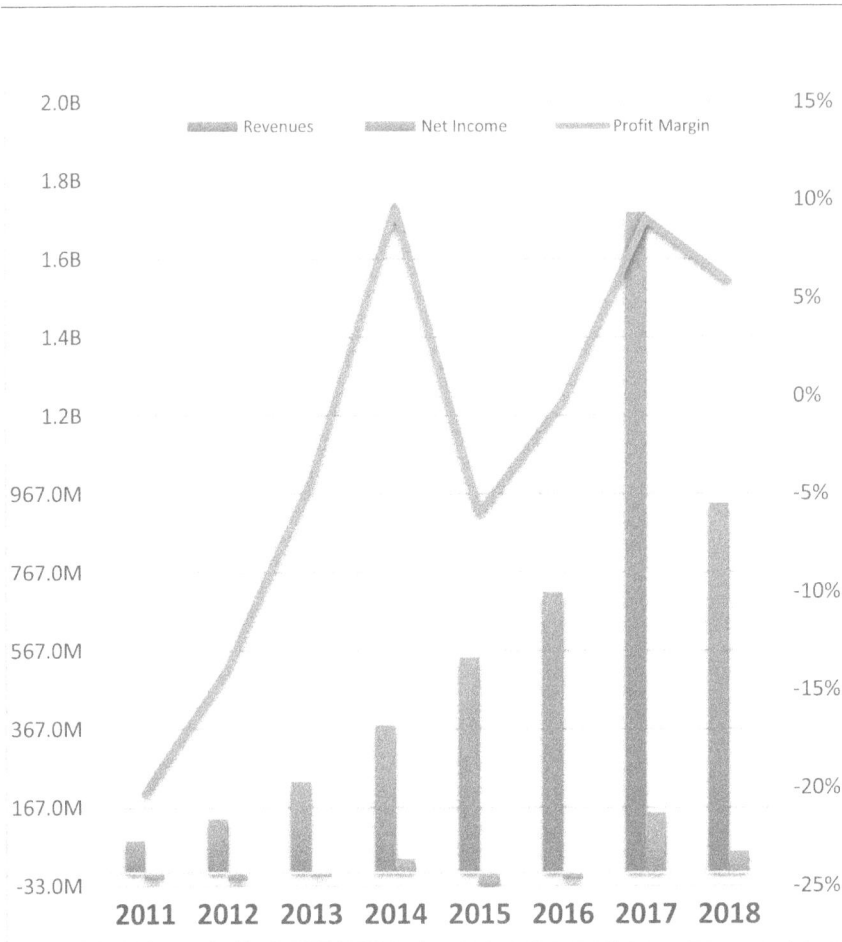

INCOME STATEMENT								
83	138	233	378	550	716	1,686	943	**Revenues**
(17)	(19)	(10)	37	(33)	(2)	153	55	**Net Income**
-20.29%	-13.88%	-4.33%	9.67%	-5.99%	-0.24%	9.08%	5.88%	**Profit Margin**
2011	2012	2013	2014	2015	2016	2017	2018	**YELP**

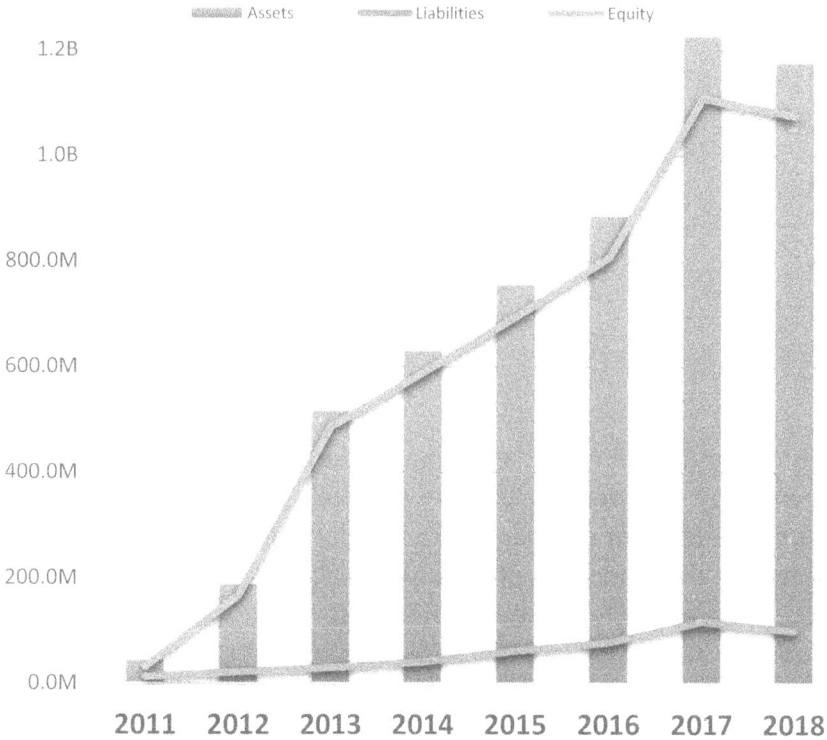

Legend: Assets — Liabilities — Equity

1.2B								
1.0B								
800.0M								
600.0M								
400.0M								
200.0M								
0.0M								
	2011	2012	2013	2014	2015	2016	2017	2018

BALANCE SHEET

44	188	516	630	755	885	1,226	1,176	**Assets**
13	22	30	42	62	78	117	100	**Liabilities**
31	166	487	588	694	807	1,109	1,076	**Equity**
15	54	66	77	75	77	87	89	**Shares** (diluted)
2.03	3.06	7.40	7.67	9.29	10.46	12.71	12.13	**Book Value** (per share)

2011 2012 2013 2014 2015 2016 2017 2018   YELP

26

ZTS

Zoetis

ZTS was founded in 2012 and is headquartered in Parsippany, New Jersey. ZTS was a subsidiary of Pfizer, Inc. and was spun-out as an independent company. ZTS is a global leader in the discovery, development, and commercialization of animal medicines, anti-infectives, vaccines, parasiticides and diagnostic products. According to ZTS's 2018 Annual Report, they provide health care products for over eight species of animals including, cattle, swine, poultry, fish, sheep, dogs, cats and horses.

ZTS has three main sources of revenue. Their largest revenue segment is livestock (51.15%), followed by companion animal (44.86%), and contract manufacturing (1.00%). Over 50.61% of ZTS's revenues are earned outside of the United States.

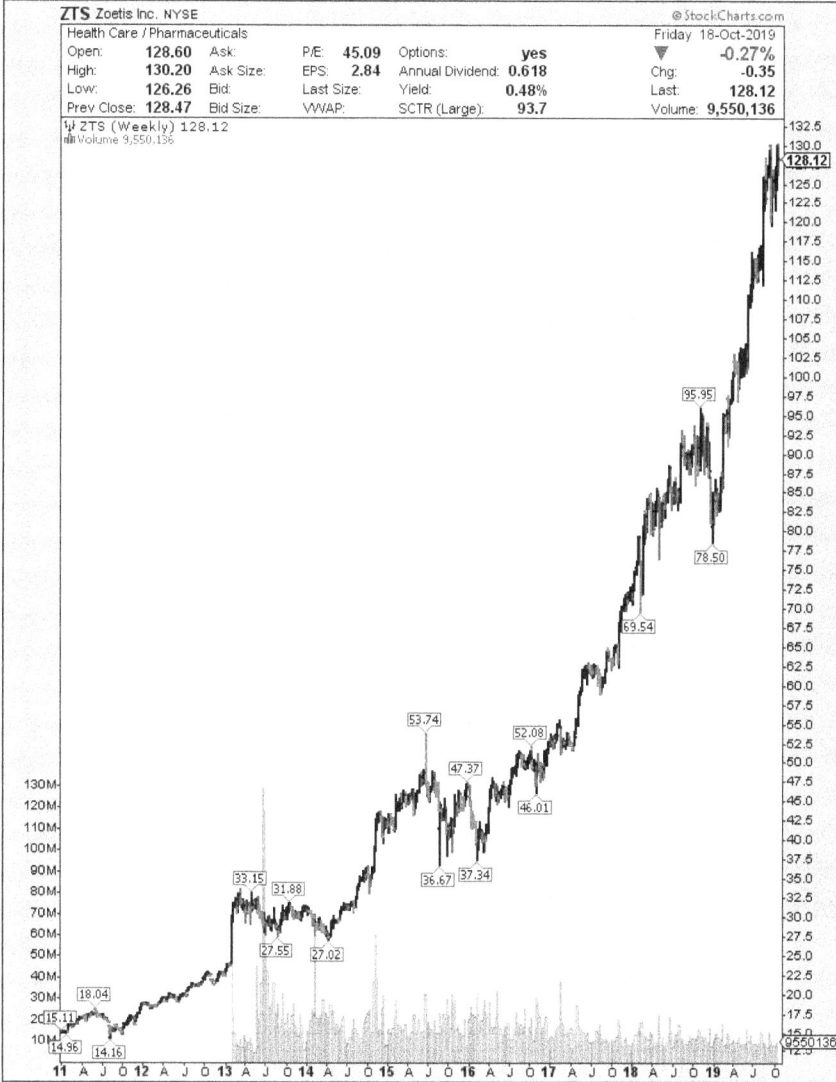

ZTS stock price chart courtesy of Stockcharts.com

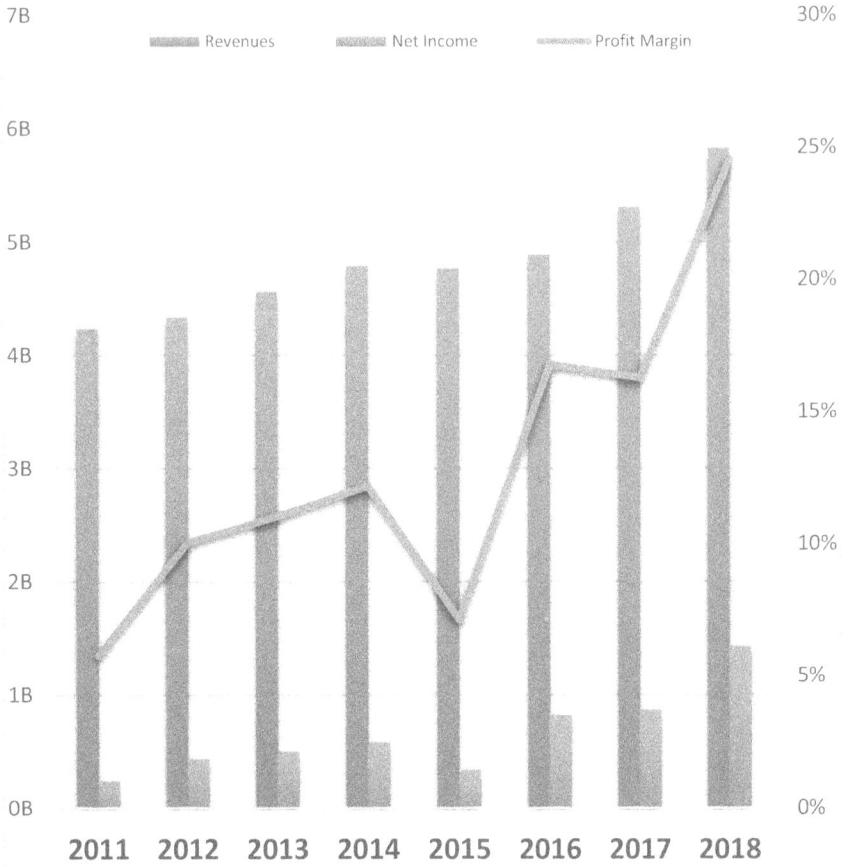

| | Revenues | Net Income | Profit Margin |

INCOME STATEMENT

4,233	4,336	4,561	4,785	4,765	4,888	5,307	5,825	Revenues
245	436	504	583	339	821	864	1,428	Net Income
5.79%	10.06%	11.05%	12.18%	7.11%	16.80%	16.28%	24.52%	Profit Margin

ZTS

Stockabet 2019:
An A Through Z Snapshot of 26 Influential Companies

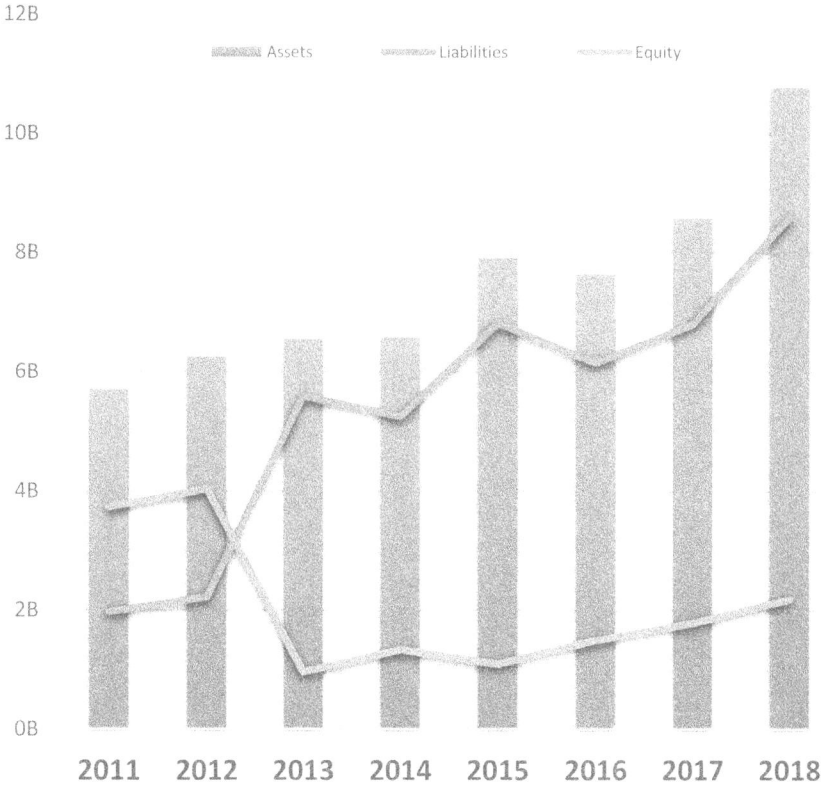

								BALANCE SHEET
5,711	6,262	6,558	6,588	7,913	7,649	8,586	10,777	**Assets**
1,975	2,221	5,596	5,251	6,822	6,150	6,800	8,592	**Liabilities**
3,736	4,041	962	1,337	1,091	1,499	1,786	2,185	**Equity**
								Shares
500	500	500	502	502	498	493	487	(diluted)
								Book Value
7.47	8.08	1.92	2.66	2.17	3.01	3.62	4.49	(per share)

About the Author

Stevan Pirkovic is a seasoned entrepreneur with a career spanning several fields, including finance, retail, politics, and most recently higher education, with one of the top research universities in the nation. Born in Flint, Michigan, Stevan earned his BBA and degree in economics from the University of Michigan-Flint. Stevan currently resides in Ann Arbor, Michigan, and in his spare time serves as a volunteer board member at his local credit union.

Once an avid investor, Stevan earned his Series 3 certification for trading commodities and futures contracts from the National Futures Association (NFA). Stevan still trades the markets but has turned his focus to market research and long-term investment strategies.

An aspiring author, Stevan decided to share his reporting on the various public companies he has been researching. His efforts led him to write this helpful snapshot of companies allowing readers to compare and contact different industries and sectors of the economy. You can connect with Stevan at Stevan@Pirkovic.com.

References

Mohan, Nishant. "Companies Are Finding More Accounting Flubs." The Wall Street Journal. Dow Jones & Company, 20 September. 2018. Web. 4 January 2020 <https://www.wsj.com/articles/companies-are-finding-more-accounting-flubs-1537474747>

Snavely, Brent. "FCA Confirms Federal Investigation into Sales Reports." Detroit Free Press. USA TODAY Network, 19 July 2016. Web. 4 January 2020. <https://www.freep.com/story/money/cars/chrysler/2016/07/18/fca-confirms-under-federal-investigation/87258690/>

Snavely, Brent. "Freep Breaks down FCA's Eye-Popping Sales Restatement." Detroit Free Press. USA TODAY Network, 27 July 2016. Web. 4 January 2020. <https://www.freep.com/story/money/cars/chrysler/2016/07/26/fcas-revealing-and-eye-popping-sales-restatement/87584484/>

Mulier, Thomas, and Craig Giammona. "Kraft Heinz Finds Procurement Misconduct, Will Restate Earnings." Bloomberg. Bloomberg L.P., 6 May 2019. Web. 11 January 2020. <https://www.bloomberg.com/news/articles/2019-05-06/kraft-heinz-to-restate-earnings-as-procurement-misconduct-found>

Elejalde-Ruiz, Alexia. "Kraft Heinz Is Correcting $181 Million in Financial Misstatements. Here's What That Means." Chicago Tribune. Tribune Media Group, 6 May 2019. Web. 11 January 2020. <https://www.chicagotribune.com/business/ct-biz-kraft-heinz-restating-earnings-20190506-story.html>

Venugopal, Aishwarya. "Kraft Heinz to Restate Nearly Three Years of Financial Reports after Investigation." Reuters. Thomson Reuters, 6 May 2019. Web. 11 January 2020. <https://www.reuters.com/article/us-kraft-heinz-restatement/kraft-heinz-to-restate-nearly-three-years-of-financial-reports-after-investigation-idUSKCN1SC0VF>

Abbott Laboratories. "Form 10-K for Fiscal Year Ended December 31, 2018." EDGAR. Securities and Exchange Commission, 22 February 2019. Web. 19 October 2019. <https://www.sec.gov/cgi-bin/browse-edgar?action=getcompany&CIK=0000001800>

Stockabet 2019:
An A Through Z Snapshot of 26 Influential Companies

Boston Properties "Form 10-K for Fiscal Year Ended December 31, 2018." EDGAR. Securities and Exchange Commission, 28 February 2019. Web. 19 October 2019. <https://www.sec.gov/cgi-bin/browse-edgar?action=getcompany&CIK=0001043121>

Colgate-Palmolive Company "Form 10-K for Fiscal Year Ended December 31, 2018." EDGAR. Securities and Exchange Commission, 21 February 2019. Web. 19 October 2019. <https://www.sec.gov/cgi-bin/browse-edgar?action=getcompany&CIK=0000021665>

Domino's Pizza. "Form 10-K for Fiscal Year Ended December 30, 2018." EDGAR. Securities and Exchange Commission, 21 February 2019. Web. 27 October 2019. <https://www.sec.gov/cgi-bin/browse-edgar?action=getcompany&CIK=0001286681>

Equity Residential. "Form 10-K for Fiscal Year Ended December 31, 2018." EDGAR. Securities and Exchange Commission, 21 February 2019. Web. 27 October 2019. <https://www.sec.gov/cgi-bin/browse-edgar?action=getcompany&CIK=0000906107>

Fidelity National Financial. "Form 10-K for Fiscal Year Ended December 31, 2018." EDGAR. Securities and Exchange Commission, 19 February 2019. Web. 2 November 2019. <https://www.sec.gov/cgi-bin/browse-edgar?action=getcompany&CIK=0001331875>

General Dynamics. "Form 10-K for Fiscal Year Ended December 31, 2018." EDGAR. Securities and Exchange Commission, 13 February 2019. Web. 2 November 2019. <https://www.sec.gov/cgi-bin/browse-edgar?action=getcompany&CIK=0000040533>

Home Depot. "Form 10-K for Fiscal Year Ended February 3, 2019." EDGAR. Securities and Exchange Commission, 28 March 2019. Web. 2 November 2019. <https://www.sec.gov/cgi-bin/browse-edgar?action=getcompany&CIK=0000354950>

IAC/Interactivecorp. "Form 10-K for Fiscal Year Ended December 31, 2018." EDGAR. Securities and Exchange Commission, 1 March 2019. Web. 9 November 2019. <https://www.sec.gov/cgi-bin/browse-edgar?action=getcompany&CIK=0000891103>

Johnson & Johnson. "Form 10-K for Fiscal Year Ended December 30, 2018." EDGAR. Securities and Exchange Commission, 20 February 2019. Web. 9 November 2019. <https://www.sec.gov/cgi-bin/browse-edgar?action=getcompany&CIK=0000200406>

Kansas City Southern. "Form 10-K for Fiscal Year Ended December 31, 2018." EDGAR. Securities and Exchange Commission, 25 January 2019. Web. 9 November 2019. <https://www.sec.gov/cgi-bin/browse-edgar?action=getcompany&CIK=0000054480>

Lockheed Martin Corporation. "Form 10-K for Fiscal Year Ended December 31, 2018." EDGAR. Securities and Exchange Commission, 8 February 2019. Web. 9 November 2019. <https://www.sec.gov/cgi-bin/browse-edgar?action=getcompany&CIK=0000936468>

Microsoft. "Form 10-K for Fiscal Year Ended June 30, 2019." EDGAR. Securities and Exchange Commission, 8 August 2019. Web. 16 November 2019. <https://www.sec.gov/cgi-bin/browse-edgar?action=getcompany&CIK=0000789019>

Nike. "Form 10-K for Fiscal Year Ended May 31, 2019." EDGAR. Securities and Exchange Commission, 23 July 2019. Web. 16 November 2019. <https://www.sec.gov/cgi-bin/browse-edgar?action=getcompany&CIK=0000320187>

Omnicom Group. "Form 10-K for Fiscal Year Ended December 31, 2018." EDGAR. Securities and Exchange Commission, 12 February 2019. Web. 16 November 2019. <https://www.sec.gov/cgi-bin/browse-edgar?action=getcompany&CIK=0000029989>

Pepsico. "Form 10-K for Fiscal Year Ended December 29, 2018." EDGAR. Securities and Exchange Commission, 15 February 2019. Web. 23 November 2019. <https://www.sec.gov/cgi-bin/browse-edgar?action=getcompany&CIK=0000077476>

Qualcomm. "Form 10-K for Fiscal Year Ended September 29, 2019." EDGAR. Securities and Exchange Commission, 6 November 2019. Web. 23 November 2019. <https://www.sec.gov/cgi-bin/browse-edgar?action=getcompany&CIK=0000804328>

Royal Caribbean Cruises. "Form 10-K for Fiscal Year Ended December 31, 2018." EDGAR. Securities and Exchange Commission, 22 February 2019. Web. 23 November 2019. <https://www.sec.gov/cgi-bin/browse-edgar?action=getcompany&CIK=0000884887>

Sinclair Broadcast Group. "Form 10-K for Fiscal Year Ended December 31, 2018." EDGAR. Securities and Exchange Commission, 1 March 2019. Web. 23 November 2019. <https://www.sec.gov/cgi-bin/browse-edgar?action=getcompany&CIK=0000912752>

Texas Instruments. "Form 10-K for Fiscal Year Ended December 31, 2018." EDGAR. Securities and Exchange Commission, 22 February 2019. Web. 30 November 2019. <https://www.sec.gov/cgi-bin/browse-edgar?action=getcompany&CIK=0000097476>

Universal Forest Products. "Form 10-K for Fiscal Year Ended December 29, 2018." EDGAR. Securities and Exchange Commission, 27 February 2019. Web. 30 November 2019. <https://www.sec.gov/cgi-bin/browse-edgar?action=getcompany&CIK=0000912767>

Verizon Communications. "Form 10-K for Fiscal Year Ended December 31, 2018." EDGAR. Securities and Exchange Commission, 15 February 2019. Web. 30 November 2019. <https://www.sec.gov/cgi-bin/browse-edgar?action=getcompany&CIK=0000732712>

Waste Management. "Form 10-K for Fiscal Year Ended December 31, 2018." EDGAR. Securities and Exchange Commission, 14 February 2019. Web. 7 December 2019. <https://www.sec.gov/cgi-bin/browse-edgar?action=getcompany&CIK=0000823768>

Xerox Holdings. "Form 10-K for Fiscal Year Ended December 31, 2018." EDGAR. Securities and Exchange Commission, 25 February 2019. Web. 7 December 2019. <https://www.sec.gov/cgi-bin/browse-edgar?action=getcompany&CIK=0000108772>

Yelp. "Form 10-K for Fiscal Year Ended December 31, 2018." EDGAR. Securities and Exchange Commission, 1 March 2019. Web. 14 December 2019. <https://www.sec.gov/cgi-bin/browse-edgar?action=getcompany&CIK=0001345016>

Zoetis. "Form 10-K for Fiscal Year Ended December 31, 2018." EDGAR.
    Securities and Exchange Commission, 14 February 2019. Web. 14
    December 2019. <https://www.sec.gov/cgi-bin/browse-
    edgar?action=getcompany&CIK=0001555280>

www.ingramcontent.com/pod-product-compliance
Lightning Source LLC
Chambersburg PA
CBHW060618210326
41520CB00010B/1390